Places for Thinking

Places for Thinking

Resource Manual

Laurance Splitter and Tim Sprod

First published 1999
by The Australian Council for Educational Research Ltd
19 Prospect Hill Road, Camberwell, Melbourne, Victoria, 3124

Edited by Barbara Burton
Designed and formatted by Francesca Partridge & Franck Dubuc
Printed by Brown Prior Anderson

National Library of Australia Cataloguing-in-Publication data:

Splitter, Laurance.
Places for thinking.
Bibliography.

ISBN 0 86431 287 3.
1. Philosophy - Study and teaching (Primary). 2. Thought and thinking - Study and teaching (Primary). I Partridge, Francesca & Dubuc, Franck. In a tree. II. Partridge, Francesca & Dubuc, Franck. On a plain.III. Partridge, Francesca & Dubuc, Franck. On a path. IV. Partridge,Francesca & Dubuc, Franck. In a field. V. Sprod, Tim. VI. Australian Council for Educational Research. VII. Title. VIII. Title : In a tree. IX. Title : On a plain. X. Title : On a path. XI. Title : In a field.

372.8

contents

Introduction

This resource manual has been designed to complement a quartet of stories, presented in picture-book format, called In a Field, On a Path, On a Plain, and In a Tree. It is written for teachers, parents and anyone else who has the time, and the interest, to sit down with children and help them to become better thinkers. The stories provide a 'way in' to a collection of questions and ideas which all thinkers — including children — should find intriguing, fascinating, puzzling and worthwhile. Picture books can be good for many reasons: they can have interesting characters, funny stories, beautiful pictures or exciting adventures. But where good thinking is the primary agenda, these aspects are not the primary focus. Important as they all undoubtedly are, they are not necessary for provoking thinking — and they are certainly not sufficient. In this manual, we concentrate on that aspect which is important: the ideas and puzzles. This resource manual has been designed to complement a quartet of stories, presented in picture-book format, called In a Field, On a Path, On a Plain, and In a Tree. It is written for teachers, parents and anyone else who has the time, and the interest, to sit down with children and help them to become better thinkers. The stories provide a 'way in' to a collection of questions and ideas which all thinkers — including children — should find intriguing, fascinating, puzzling and worthwhile. Picture books can be good for many reasons: they can have interesting characters, funny stories, beautiful pictures or exciting adventures. But where good thinking is the primary agenda, these aspects are not the primary focus. Important as they all undoubtedly are, they are not necessary for provoking thinking — and they are certainly not sufficient. In this manual, we concentrate on that aspect which is important: the ideas and puzzles. This resource manual has been designed to complement a quartet of stories, presented in picture-book format, called In a Field, On a Path, On a Plain, and In a Tree. It is written for teachers, parents and anyone else who has the time, and the interest, to sit down with children and help them to become better thinkers. The stories provide a 'way in' to a collection of questions and ideas which all thinkers — including children — should find intriguing, fascinating, puzzling and worthwhile. Picture books can be good for many reasons: they can have interesting characters, funny stories, beautiful pictures or exciting adventures. But where good thinking is the primary agenda, these aspects are not the primary focus. Important as they all undoubtedly are, they are not necessary for provoking thinking — and they are certainly not sufficient. In this manual, we concentrate on that aspect which is important: the ideas and puzzles. This resource manual has been designed to complement a quartet of stories, presented in picture-book format, called In a Field, On a Path, On a Plain, and In a Tree. It is written for teachers, parents and anyone else who has the time, and the interest, to sit down with children and help them to become better thinkers. The stories provide a 'way

This resource manual has been designed to complement a quartet of stories, presented in picture-book format, called *In a field, On a path, On a plain,* and *In a tree*. It is written for teachers, parents and anyone else who has the time, and the interest, to sit down with children and help them to become better thinkers. The stories provide a 'way in' to a collection of questions and ideas which all thinkers — including children — should find intriguing, fascinating, puzzling and worthwhile. Picture books can be good for many reasons: they can have interesting characters, funny stories, beautiful pictures or exciting adventures. But where good thinking is the primary agenda, these aspects are not the primary focus. Important as they all undoubtedly are, they are not necessary for provoking thinking — and they are certainly not sufficient. In this manual, we concentrate on that aspect which is important: the ideas and puzzles.

The manual has been organised into five sections: the introduction and a section for each of the books. The latter four sections are themselves split into subsections, each of which deals with one of the 'big ideas' raised by that book. These are called the 'leading ideas'. Throughout this introduction, we shall be talking generally about the approaches that you can take in using these four picture books to promote children's thinking. We shall touch on ideas which are treated in further detail under one or more of the 'leading ideas'. At these times, we will refer you to the associated leading ideas, which are identified as follows: *Tree* 3 refers to leading idea 3 for the book *In a tree*.

In the leading ideas, we have identified some questions that children are likely to ask, and provided some cues for further inquiry through discussion plans, exercises and activities. But we recommend that the primary source of questions and ideas be the children themselves. Encouraging children to think about what it is that most interests them is an important part of working as a *community of inquiry*.

A glance at the stories themselves will reveal many of the ideas that are followed up in this manual. A recurring theme is that of *thinking* itself — cows which ruminate and ponder, snails which imagine and wonder, a duck which realises and reasons, a giraffe which feels bored and tries to see the world from an ant's point of view... With just a little encouragement, these scenarios will move children to talk endlessly about what 'thinking' really means and, in so doing, become more aware of *how well* they are thinking and how they might work to improve their thinking. As an integral part of this process, they also become more aware of how their friends think. They discover, among other things, that when they think about a question or an idea together — for this is what communal inquiry is all about — they are likely to come up with new and exciting thoughts. [See *Field* 5, 6; *Path* 1]

An essential component of inquiry is the interweaving of *thinking* and *talking*. Through learning to engage in collaborative dialogue, young children find an outlet for their thinking — a way of expressing what they think and feel about things — which would otherwise not be available to them. Conversely, the dialogue itself informs and activates their thinking. We could say that just as the community of inquiry is a place where children can 'think out loud', so too their thinking increasingly takes the form of 'internalised dialogue'.

In the few years just before and after they start school, children commonly talk to themselves as they engage in tasks — using the sort of dialogue that they have had with others to guide themselves. As they grow older, this talk gradually becomes more and more quiet and terse. Eventually, it goes 'underground' as inner speech or verbal thought.

It is not just the beginnings of verbal thought that arise in spoken interaction between the child and others. Throughout childhood, and probably throughout life, the tasks that we can jointly accomplish by talking together are gradually internalised as tasks that we can achieve on our own by thinking them through. This is one of the core insights that underlies Philosophy for Children, and it rests on work done by the Russian psychologist, Lev Vygotsky, and the American philosopher, George Herbert Mead, in the early part of the century.

So one of the most important tasks for you, as the teacher, in running a discussion in your classroom, is to try to ensure that the quality of the discussion is kept high enough to extend the children's thinking, without pushing it so high that the children lose touch. This level of discussion, where the children are thinking together, with your support, at a higher level than they could manage individually, was called by Vygotsky the Zone of Proximal Development.

Of course, we are not advocating that you share this learning theory with your students. Nevertheless, we do think that children can focus directly on their own thoughts, and the similarity between thinking, talking to oneself and talking together. Talking about how they are thinking will lead, in the same manner, to thinking about how they are thinking. Such metacognition, as it is called, is widely recognised as an important ingredient in the quality of children's thinking. [See *Path* 7; *Plain* 5]

In picture books, of course, it is not only the words which can be puzzling or interesting — the pictures can also raise questions in children's minds. At a number of places, we have provided suggestions for inquiry based on the visual content of the stories. [See *Path* 5; *Plain* 10; *Tree* 7]

What is this community of inquiry? We prefer to think of it as a kind of classroom environment in which the process of interweaving between thinking and talking is the main focus. It is a place where children think, talk, reason and listen together. It is a place where everyone's ideas are valued as potential sources of truth and understanding. It is a secure and safe place in which children trust one another sufficiently — as well as the teacher — to 'try out' new ideas and exercise their creative thinking capacities. It is a place where children learn to look for and respect alternative perspectives (rather than just accept one fixed view of things) and in so doing realise that there is nothing wrong with changing your mind and thinking again. It is an environment which builds self-esteem because it allows children to see themselves as thinkers who can 'make a difference'. [See *Tree* 6]

Philosophy and philosophical thinking *Places for Thinking* has been written to supplment the growing literature in *Philosophy for Children* — specifically for children in the first four years of school. But what do we mean by 'philosophical thinking'? Here are three ways of answering this question.

- Philosophical thinking is 'thinking about thinking, in ways which help us improve our thinking'. When children do philosophy, they not only engage in a broad range of thinking processes; they do this *self-consciously* or *reflectively*. In other words, they become more aware of themselves as thinkers. Further, they develop a sense of what is involved in improving their thinking: giving good reasons for their opinions, asking probing questions, building on each other's ideas, being aware of the direction that a particular topic is taking and sticking to the point, recognising that there is almost always more than one way to think about something … In this way they develop and strengthen their capacity for good *judgement*.

Encouraging children to think about thinking (including the different words and expressions we use to describe thinking) is one way of opening up for them the power and richness of their own minds. The books themselves contain numerous words to describe different types of thinking. You can ask children to identify them, and discuss the differences between them, at any stage.

The 'reflective' or metacognitive turn in philosophy is a powerful device when it comes to helping children improve their thinking. In practice, it has the peculiar effect of turning the investigation back onto itself. For example, a student who challenges her friend to provide a good reason for her view might be called upon to explain what she means by good reason in that context. This gives philosophical inquiry its characteristic 'double edge': there is the first-order focus on the subject at hand, and there is, interwoven with this focus, a second-order focus on the method of inquiry itself. So it is not just a matter of asking 'What are we talking about here?', but 'How well are we talking about it, and how could we do it better?'. It is the discipline of philosophy which makes room for asking and examining these second-order questions.

- Philosophical thinking is 'thinking about concepts and ideas'. In one sense, any concept is ripe for philosophical investigation, but it would be more helpful to point to a cluster of concepts which have intrigued and fascinated philosophers for several thousand years. Such concepts include: being a person; mind and thinking; real vs imaginary; space and time; what it means to be good, or fair, or just; the nature of beauty; what makes something true. There is, in part, a historical component here: these concepts are age-old and yet still continue to puzzle anyone who cares to think about them. But it is not just their history which makes them philosophical. Philosophical concepts may be characterised as concepts which are:

common to the experiences of most people (including children) in the ordinary course of their lives;

central to the task of giving meaning to, or making sense of, these every-day experiences;

contestable or problematic, in that their meanings are never completely resolved.

The concepts which lie just beneath the surface of the four picture books which make up *Places for Thinking* meet these conditions. Children are intensely interested in questions about the 'why' and 'wherefore' of things — provided that such questions are presented in ways which are accessible and attractive to them. It is worth remembering the words of Aristotle: 'Philosophy begins in wonder'. Here we have an immediate affinity between children and philosophy, because children, too, can be inspired to think through wonder. [See *Field* 10]

- Philosophical thinking is 'dialogical thinking' and, hence, focused on the thinking of many people, rather than the thinking of a single individual. True, we have all heard about those philosophers (like René Descartes) who did their most creative and powerful thinking while locked in a room by themselves, but when it comes to developing a philosophical culture among children, we should rather follow a different paradigm, like Socrates: that of the *community of inquiry* working together to unravel and make sense of those questions and concepts which puzzle and intrigue us. [See *Field* 8; *Tree* 2, 6]

Tips and strategies for using this manual

- Give your students access to the philosophical questions and activities contained in the manual through sharing with them the stories and illustrations. Remember, the manual is designed to help you identify the leading ideas and structure philosophical discussion around them, but the picture books themselves are for the children. They provide a launching pad for your students to embark on their journey of philosophical exploration and discovery.

- If the children (or some of them) can read, encourage them to share the story by reading around in a circle. If they can't read out loud, help them or read it to them.

- Once they have read one of the stories and explored the illustrations, ask them to think about anything there that they might have found interesting. Encourage them to articulate their concerns in the form of questions or statements which you can put up on the board or on butcher's paper (so that the questions gathered can be retained for future use). Put next to each question the name of the child who raised it, to emphasise that it is his or her question (which they are now contributing to the community as a whole).

- Help the children organise their questions and choose one or more with which to begin a discussion.

- Guide them in a discussion of their questions, utilising the ideas and activities in the manual to assist in giving a 'philosophical focus' to the task. This is perhaps the most challenging task for you. Below, we provide some further guidance as to how to achieve this, but we also recommend that you take advantage of training provided by Philosophy for Children organisations (see the Appendix for a contact address) or read some of the excellent books about Philosophy for Children that are available (also listed in the Appendix).

- Encourage children to be aware of the structure and direction of their own inquiry, by asking such questions as:

  'Do you think we are getting closer to answering the question?',
  'Can you connect your comment to what she said?',

'Are you agreeing with her and disagreeing with him?',
'Can anyone provide an example or a counter-example to what she said?',
'Do you think his reasons for saying that are good ones?',

and so on. Good questioning here is partly a matter of technique but also a matter of philosophical acumen. The commentaries and discussion plans provided under the leading ideas are designed to help you sensitise yourself to the philosophical issues, so it is a good idea to have read and digested them before using the book with your students.

Getting started: Building thinking; Building the community

You can eventually turn your class into an experienced community of inquiry made up of experienced thinkers, but obviously this is going to take some time. At first, your class will not be a fully-fledged community of inquiry for two reasons: students will not have developed the necessary tools for good thinking skills; and they will not yet have developed the ability to work together as a community. One of our key claims is that these two developments take place hand in hand. It is through thinking together that the children learn to think individually — that is, to think for themselves.

So when you begin to build a community of inquiry in your class, your students are going to need a lot of assistance from you to build these attributes. This is a delicate task because, if the class is going eventually to form a community of inquiry, you cannot be too directive and do all the work yourself. If you do, they will never be able to take over the community and direct it themselves. On the other hand, if you are not directive enough, the community will lack focus and not develop beyond a disjointed conversation. One way to help ensure that you do not take too much control is to allow the children to ask the questions for inquiry, right from the start, in their own words. The agenda for discussion will then always be theirs.

Nevertheless, there are a number of steps that you can take to help equip your students for the community of inquiry. In the early weeks of building a thinking community, you will probably need to be more directive than you will be later, and more directive with younger children than with older ones, while being careful not to impose your own views on the discussion. The steps can be roughly divided into those that build thinking and those that build the community. The notes below are designed to draw your attention to some of these areas. Each of them is treated in greater detail elsewhere throughout the leading ideas. Here, we are concerned to focus on their importance in the early stages of the community.

Building thinking

Questions Your children may or may not be clear about the difference between a question and a statement, and this may depend on their age. When asked what puzzles or interests them, kindergarten children will often make a statement about the story, or echo something that was said in it ('I liked it when …'; 'The cat did such-and-such'). They may not be able to reformulate this as a question that pinpoints the issue that they want addressed. By Year 1 or 2, many children will be more able to do this.

You can assist children to hone this most important skill in several ways. One is to ask the rest of the class to assist the first child by suggesting questions that arise from the comment. If no-one in the class can do so, you can suggest some questions yourself. Focusing on the 'question words' can help (who, what, where, how, why, when). Inviting the child who made the comment to talk a little more about it can also clarify the question that lies behind it. Another fun exercise is to make a statement (e.g. 'His name was Fred') and ask the children to give you as many questions as they can to which the statement could be an answer (e.g. 'What was his name?'; 'Who stole the cookie jar?' etc.). You should find, over time, that more children will ask questions rather than make comments. This is certainly an advance that you want to encourage, but do not try to force it to happen too quickly. [See *Field* 1; *Tree* 4]

Reasons Early on, children are very likely to make their contributions to the dialogue in the form of bald assertions. Central to reasoning, of course, is that we give reasons for our assertions. Children need practice at this. Many of the discussion plans and exercises in this manual revolve around the seeking of reasons, so it is often useful in a young community to have some explicit practice at giving reasons. You can start by asking children to give their opinions about some open-ended matter, and to back up their opinion with a reason.

For example, when you have read *On a plain*, you might ask the children what sort of animal they would have liked to try being, if they were the giraffe. As each gives a different animal, ask them to give a reason why they chose that animal. Encourage them to move from 'I think that …' towards 'I think that … because …' As children become better at this, you can encourage others to react to such assertions: 'I agree with Rory, because …', or 'I disagree with Julia because …' You are working towards the stage when children will automatically give a reason for any assertion, but you may need to keep asking 'Why do you say that?' or something similar for quite a long time before this becomes second nature. [See *Path* 9; *Tree* 5]

Sameness, similarity and difference A central concern of many of the leading ideas that arise in this manual is finding ways in which apparently disparate things are the same, and apparently identical things are different. For example, we explore how being an animal is like being a human, or how wondering and imagining are different. Thinking clearly very often depends on recognising connections or important distinctions. Much of our reasoning works through finding similarities. Similes, metaphors and analogies all depend on noting ways in which things that are apparently different are similar, and to use them properly also needs an appreciation of how, despite these similarities, they still differ. Indeed, if we look closely at our language, we find that much of it is metaphorical. In fact, the previous sentence works because of an analogy between using our eyes to look at an object, and using our minds to 'look' at an abstract entity, for example.

One very important type of sameness and difference exists in the meanings of words. On the one hand, two different words may mean much the same thing (they are synonyms). An example explored in this manual is the similarity of 'thinking' and 'talking to yourself'. Interestingly, even synonyms such as these often differ, not in their primary or core meaning, but in the connotations that they have. For example, 'spinster' and 'unmarried woman' may mean the same, but the word 'spinster' carries an extra layer of meaning. On the other hand, one word can have two meanings. An example discussed later in the manual is the word 'interest'. Ambiguity, which often arises from double meanings, is also very important to thinking. If we are unaware that a word may be being used in two different senses, we can go very wrong.

Early in the building of a community, you should be aware of opportunities to ask children to recognise sameness and difference in their discussions ('How is that the same as …?'; 'How does that differ from …?'), and you might find that it is very helpful to choose discussion plans and exercises that build the skills of recognising sameness and difference.

Connections and arguments To learn a language is (at least in part) to learn to make connections between statements; that is, to learn how arguments work. It is important to be clear here about what we mean by 'argument'. What we have in mind is not people quarrelling or shouting at each other. Rather, what we mean by an argument is a sequence of statements which are connected, in that the truth (or plausibility) of the earlier statements lead us to accept the truth (or plausibility) of the later ones.

Some of the most important words in the language are the little words that do this work of connecting statements and ideas. We have in mind words like 'if', 'then', 'so', 'but', 'because', 'all', 'some', 'no'. These are sometimes referred to as the 'logical' words, because logic depends so heavily on their proper use. Now, we are not suggesting that your children can, or should, be formally taught logic. But to learn to use these little words correctly is of vital importance to their future ability to reason well. So we suggest that you are aware of the ways in which children do use these words, and that you take the opportunities presented to explore them.

As examples, we shall outline three basic types of argument. The first is 'if … then …' reasoning. You will notice that the word 'if' appears often in this manual, and some leading ideas depend heavily on it (e.g. *Path* 4: 'If I had a voice'). Children are usually reasonably good at the first sort of reasoning that uses 'if … then …' Let's take the statement 'If you touch a hot stove, then you will feel pain'. Given the truth of this statement, children are good at deciding the outcome of touching a hot stove.

A second type of reasoning can be called 'part-whole' reasoning. An example would be 'Fido is a dog. A dog is an animal. Therefore Fido is an animal'. If each of the first two sentences is true, then the third must also be true. This is because Fido is part of the group of dogs, and dogs are part of the group of animals. From this we can see that Fido must also be part of the group of animals.

A third type of reasoning to be aware of is generalisation. Here's an example: 'Daffy Duck has webbed feet. Donald Duck has webbed feet. Daisy Duck has webbed feet. Therefore all ducks have webbed feet'. As you can see, this sort of reasoning is not as strongly conclusive as the previous two. For example, Europeans saw many white swans in Europe and concluded that all swans are white. When they came to Australia, however, it only took one look at the black swans here to show that their reasoning was unsound. Nevertheless, generalising is a very important type of reasoning, because it is the way that much of our knowledge has been built up. Children need to become aware both of its power and its pitfalls.

Building the community

Talking one at a time One of the more difficult tasks you might have at first is getting the children to talk one at a time, especially when the conversation becomes interesting and exciting. Yet if they cannot do this, then the discussion will break down. There are several strategies you can use to help the children here. At first, you will probably need to insist on 'hands up', and choose the next speaker yourself. Indeed, you probably use this technique already. However, as the community builds, a strict insistence on 'hands' can be counter-productive. It inhibits the students from attending to each other properly (see below) and enforces a teacher-student-teacher-student pattern of interaction, rather than encouraging a more naturally flowing dialogue.

You might like to experiment with a 'speaking object', such as a toy or a cush ball. This is an object that must be held by the speaker, and then passed to the next speaker. Only the child (or teacher!) who is holding the object is permitted to speak. You can play a role in directing who it goes to next, or leave that decision to the child holding it. You also need to exercise some judgement about the extent to which you yourself may not speak without it. While the 'speaking object' can make children more aware of the possibilities of conversing directly with each other, rather than always talking through the teacher, it also (like 'hands') has the potential to inhibit the flow of the dialogue.

Finally, you will probably be aiming for an unmediated, natural conversational dynamic in the class, where children take turns without outside direction. The skill to be able to do this is difficult to learn, especially in a large group, not only for young children but for all of us. But it is well worth working hard to try to achieve it. Its achievement depends on the following three points as well, so we shall turn our attention to them.

Listening to each other It is important that each child listens carefully to what the others are saying. Indeed, it is probably this close and attentive listening that is as (if not more) important in the building of thinking skills as is speaking in the group. Young children can be very restless, and while fidgeting is not always incompatible with listening, it will be part of your job to encourage close listening. One way to try to build this is to ask each child who wants to speak to connect their statement or question to that of previous speakers. If the children are showing little sign of listening to each other, it can be useful for a while to insist that they give a brief summary of what the previous speaker said before they are allowed to make their own point.

Connecting their statements Young children can have a tendency to say whatever pops into their minds, whether it is relevant to the discussion or not. Often, there is a connection, but it is more of the nature of a random association than a building of the inquiry. It will be one of your jobs to assist children to make connections to the whole conversation. One way to encourage this is to ask a child who makes a statement which does not seem to be well connected to expand on how the statement helps with answering the question. Alternatively, when one child says something that seems to agree, or disagree, with another child's statement, you can ask them if they are saying the same as (or something different from) what that child said ('Are you agreeing/disagreeing with Katie, then?'). Another tactic is to model and encourage statements of the type 'Sue said … but I think …', or 'I agree with Harry because …' or 'Jenny is partly right, I think, but what about …'

Showing respect The community is not only a place for sorting out ideas. If it is to really be a community, then the ideas need to be built in common. This requires that all the children see themselves as working together, and that implies that they show respect for each other, and for each other's ideas. This does not mean that all ideas are accepted equally, of course. Some ideas are better than others, and if progress is going to be made, then these better ideas will need to be acknowledged and developed, while other ideas which are not so good need to be rethought. Often, these ideas, although they may be inadequate in some way, nevertheless contain an insightful element. In any case, children should be encouraged to have intellectual humility, so that they can let go of their ideas in the face of good reasons for doing so.

The matter of showing respect for persons and for ideas is not straightforward. It is often said that children should 'attack the idea, not the person who holds the idea'. Certainly there is a lot of truth in this but, particularly with young children, this ignores the extent to which our ideas are important to us — so important in some cases that an attack on our ideas *is* an attack on us. This is not true of all our ideas, of course. In a community of inquiry, many of the ideas we put forward are not particularly important to us, and we may be well aware that we are just trying them out, and are not strongly attached to them. An attack on an idea of this sort will not be taken as devastating to us.

Teachers who know that the respect accorded to a child's ideas is important to the child's self-esteem often take this to mean that every idea a child expresses ought to be praised. Consequently, studies of teacher discourse in classrooms show that most student statements elicit an immediate evaluation from the teacher, many of which are praise. But to praise every statement can be seen as a lack of respect for the children. If weak or wrong statements are praised, then the child is denied the feedback that can lead to improvement. What's more, such an authoritative evaluation of the statement will not leave room for challenges, reflection and exploration of it.

Hence, your role in the community of inquiry is a delicate one calling for discretion and good judgement. Teachers in the community are often advised to refrain from immediate evaluation of children's statements, and we agree that this is generally a good idea. The community itself can provide more meaningful feedback. If the other children agree with something one child said, or build on it in the discussion, this will show its worth in a more meaningful manner. This does not mean that the teacher should refrain from all evaluation. To highlight examples of good ideas or reasoning is important in helping children to identify these in the future. If the other children do not recognise it, you ought to. Equally, the imperatives of self-esteem are important, and you may choose to encourage a reluctant speaker with praise. Such judgements are part and parcel of teaching.

Further, you should be sensitive to the ways in which children show respect for each other, and each other's ideas. Encourage explicit approval of ideas by other children, but also encourage disagreement — or, at least, some questioning or challenging — if it is backed by good reasons. Encourage children to recognise the difference between an attack on them, and an attack on the idea they have expressed. Equally, try to encourage those who do attack an idea to show a sensitivity in the way they make an attack. Both 'That's rubbish!' and 'I don't think that's right, because it doesn't …' can be responses to a hare-brained idea. But the former is much more likely to be interpreted as a personal attack.

Young children are prone to see things from their own point of view only. This is not necessarily because they are narrow-minded, but because they do not have much practice in putting themselves in other's shoes. The community of inquiry is a way for children to hear the views of others, and to take them seriously. In this way, children can learn how to take different perspectives on a matter.

For this to happen, we need to encourage two things simultaneously. First, children must be encouraged to speak up about their views, to take risks in opening up their thoughts to others. Secondly, they need to be humble about those thoughts, seeing them as possibilities, not certainties, that may need to be modified. Thus, you will need to make the community a safe place. When children feel comfortable, they are more likely to take the sort of intellectual, moral and emotional risks that lead to deep thinking and learning. [See *Tree* 6]

Summary

As your classroom community of inquiry builds, you may find that the need for you to be directive lessens, but it will not disappear altogether. Remember, you are in the position of being the apprentice master to your students' apprenticeship in inquiry and thinking. While the children need considerable help when they are inexperienced, you need gradually to hand over to them as their abilities and their practice develop. Let them try out their burgeoning skills and step in to support them only as and when they need it.

Assessment and evaluation

Evaluating a philosophical conversation is not a simple matter. The traditional methodology of looking for 'right answers' does not work well here. For one thing, finding solutions to philosophical problems is only one of the tasks that students in philosophy undertake (they also try to sharpen their understanding of the problem; identify and analyse key concepts; come up with insightful examples and counter-examples; make pertinent distinctions and connections; and so on). Secondly, it is not at all clear what constitutes a 'solution' in philosophy, just because philosophical problems and questions are extremely tenacious: whatever solution we come up with gives rise to still more questions and puzzles. (This is not to say that every answer in philosophy is as good as every other answer: we can help our students develop criteria for judging which of their responses and tentative solutions are productive and helpful.) Thirdly, Philosophy for Children is essentially a collaborative enterprise, in which communal activities such as dialogue and building on ideas are intrinsic. Accordingly, any form of evaluation should, in some way, reflect and represent this communal aspect.

With these provisos in mind, it is nonetheless important for teachers and students to engage in some kind of evaluation or assessment. After all, if we think that philosophy is important because it helps students to become better thinkers, better listeners, better communicators, etc., then we should be able to measure, or at least assess, such improvement.

Teachers of Philosophy for Children are devising and experimenting with a range of techniques for assessment. Taking into account the features identified earlier, the following points may assist you in this task.

Assessing thinking Ask yourself, and the classroom community, the following questions:

1. Are we/students giving each other reasons for our views?
2. Are we/they being careful about our/their assumptions?
3. Are we aware of what our views imply — where they might lead us?
4. Are we/they giving appropriate examples and counter-examples?
5. Are we/they asking good questions?
6. Did we/they show a willingness to 'self-correct' (change our/their minds)?

Assessing content

1. Did the discussion or activity have a clear focus? (Did we know what we were talking about)?
2. Did we/they stick to the point or wander all over the place?
3. Did we/they build on one another's ideas?
4. Did we/they develop new understandings or ways of looking at an issue?
5. Did we make progress with (any of) the questions we set for ourselves?

Assessing the community of inquiry

1. Did we/they listen to each other?
2. Did we/they respect each other?
3. Were we/they able to disagree with one another?
4. Is the community a 'safe place' where we/they can try out new ideas?
5. Did we/they engage in dialogue with each other (not just through the teacher)?
6. Did all those who wanted to participate find a way to do so?
7. Are any of us/them not involved or not participating? What can we do about this?

In keeping with the democratic nature of the community of inquiry, try, as possible, to engage the students in the process of their own assessment. While it may be necessary to assess individuals (and even assign grades), the community should learn to evaluate its own progress — that is, its own progress in developing and growing as a community of inquiry.

We believe strongly that teachers have both the right and the responsibility to exercise their own professional judgement (in collaboration with colleagues and, as we indicated, the children themselves) in matters of student assessment and evaluation. This does not mean that assessment in philosophy should be an entirely subjective matter — based on how teachers 'feel' about particular students — but it does underscore the importance of judgement and reminds us that quantitative or 'paper and pen' forms of testing will not usually be appropriate.

In a field

In a field a black and white cow ruminated some big questions like "why is grass green?"and "is it still green at night?"but couldn't find any answers. In a field another black and white cow pondered,"why is the sun round?" and "how can it be measured?" In a field yet another black and white cow chewed slowly, thinking of her stomachs and wanted to know why she had four rather than three or five. In a field another black and white cow, conscious of her markings mused, "what's the use of being mottled like this rather than having horizontal stripes?" By chance a passing duck was able to resolve the question asked by the last cow. In a field, by bringing them together the duck realised that these cows were born to be geography teachers and should leave the philosophy to one side...for the moment. In a field a black and white cow ruminated some big questions like "why is grass green?"and "is it still green at night?"but couldn't find any answers. In a field another black and white cow pondered, "why is the sun round?" and "how can it be measured?" In a field yet another black and white cow chewed slowly, thinking of her stomachs and wanted to know why she had four rather than three or five. In a field another black and white cow, conscious of her markings mused, "what's the use of being mottled like this rather than having horizontal stripes?" By chance a passing duck was able to resolve the question asked by the last cow. In a field, by bringing them together the duck realised that these cows were born to be geography teachers and should leave the philosophy to one side...for the moment. In a field a black and white cow ruminated some big questions like "why is grass green?"and "is it still green at night?"but couldn't find any answers. In a field another black and white cow pondered, "why is the sun round?" and "how can it be measured?" In a field yet another black and white cow chewed slowly, thinking of her stomachs and wanted to know why she had four rather than three or five. In a field another black and white cow, conscious of her markings mused, "what's the use of being mottled like this rather than having horizontal stripes?" By chance a passing duck was able to resolve the question asked by the last cow. In a field, by bringing them together the duck realised that these cows were born to be geography teachers and should leave the philosophy to one side...for the moment. IIn a field a black and white cow ruminated some big questions like "why is grass green?"and "is it still green at night?"but couldn't find any answers. In a field another black and white cow pondered, "why is the sun round?" and "how can it be measured?" In a field yet another black and white cow chewed slowly, thinking of her stomachs and wanted to know why she had four rather than three or five. In a field another black and white cow, conscious of her markings mused, "what's the use of being mottled like this rather than having horizontal stripes?" By chance a passing duck was able to resolve the question asked by the last cow. In a field, by bringing them together the duck realised that these cows were born to be geo-

Leading idea 1: Big questions

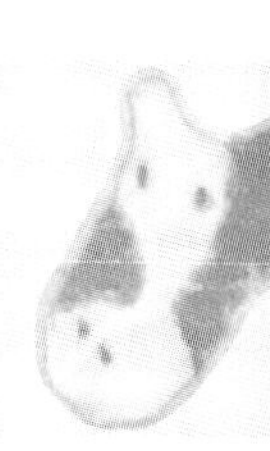

The black and white cows are asking themselves some 'big questions'. You could ask your students what they think a big question is, but it might be a good idea to begin by asking them what they think a *question* is in the first place. Perhaps they will tell you that a question is like a request: it's when you *ask* someone for something. Alternatively, they might suggest that a question is a sentence or saying that needs an answer. The important point here is that we should not assume that students (especially very young children) have a clear grasp of the concept of a question — either in syntactic (i.e. grammatical) terms or semantic (i.e. 'meaning') terms. One of the aims of this program is to help children transform their intuitive expressions of wonder, curiosity and puzzlement into questions — preferably ones that invite some serious thinking rather than a quick response from the teacher or a 'bright' student.

Then there is the question of what makes a question BIG. Some students might not think that the questions the cows ask ('Why is grass green?', 'Why is the sun round?', 'How can it be measured?') are big — after all, they haven't got many words in them, and the words themselves are not big. Perhaps they will start to see them as big once they try to answer them, or even try to work out how they might *go about* answering them. This suggests that a big question is one which contains or refers to a big idea — which, of course, shifts the focus to what we might mean by 'big idea'.

Thinking about how to answer a question raises the question of whether all questions have answers. Maybe there are questions that do have answers, but complete answers will never be known.

It is worth commenting here that children tend to classify questions in one of two ways: either they are expressions of their own ignorance (as when they ask an adult who is supposed to know the answer), or else they are devices used by teachers — who already know the answers anyway — to test out what students know and what they don't. But children can also be encouraged to ask questions which are not so much expressions of ignorance as *invitations* to think: to wonder, reflect and inquire. Perhaps so called big questions are like this: they are inviting us to think and talk together about something important.

Given the importance of questions and the role they play in thinking and learning, it is no accident that this manual is full of questions for your students to consider. We hope that they will use the stimulus provided by the accompanying stories to ask many more questions — particularly those of the invitational or inquiry kind. [See also *Tree* 4]

Activity: Asking questions

Show the children a large photograph or picture, preferably one which is intriguing or puzzling in some way. Invite them to ask as many questions as they can about it. You may need to help them formulate a question once they have found something which puzzles or interests them.

Exercise: Big questions

Ask your students whether they think the following are big questions or not. You might need to provide some examples in each case.

	Big question	Not a big question	Not sure
1. A question with a lot of words in it.			
2. A question with large letters, like this: 'What is your name?'			
3. A question with words in it that you don't understand.			
4. A question which is easy to understand but hard to answer (like, maybe, the first cow's questions).			
5. A question which has more than one answer.			
6. A question which is about a big idea.			

Exercise: Silly questions

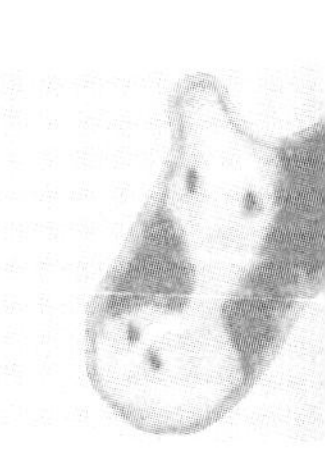

Ask your students what, if anything, is wrong with the following questions.

1. How many fish are in the butcher's shop?
2. Would you rather have a krump or a blatt?
3. How old is someone who is exactly five years old?
4. Why is the who, what, when?
5. __________(member of the class), why do you have sixteen arms?
6. How tall is a person?
7. What is the difference between a duck?
8. How long have you been sucking your foot?

Leading idea 2: Colours

The first black and white cow is asking why the grass is green. (She could also have asked why her milk is white, or why some of her relatives are brown instead of black and white). Except for those who are colour-blind, every child has some experience of colours: they see coloured things around them, they watch colour television, they draw with coloured pencils and crayons. But, as with many familiar experiences, when we begin to 'dig a little deeper' into what colours actually are, things are not quite so simple. What exactly *are* colours? Is a colour like *red* something which is inside a red pencil, or inside a can of red paint? Or are colours not really *in* things at all? But if they are not, then where, if anywhere, are they? In the mind, perhaps? Would that mean that our thoughts are coloured?

Scientists have discovered that colours can be described, in physical terms, as wave-lengths of different magnitudes. This is not something which young children would normally be interested in, but it might be of interest to teachers to think about the connection between the scientific account of colours and the puzzle about where colours 'really are'.

A very old philosophical puzzle concerns the *experience* of seeing a colour. There is a quality to that experience that is not easy to explain to others — how would you describe the experience of seeing a colour to a blind person? The only way to learn how to use colour words seems to be by pointing. So we teach children the colours by saying, e.g. 'The colour of this thing is blue'. Thus, we attach the word 'blue' to whatever experience we have when we see things that everyone else calls blue. Given this, children can wonder whether the actual experience that I have when I look at that object is the *same* as the one you have. Mightn't it be the case that your *experience* of blue is different from mine — say, the same as I would have if I looked at a red object — even though we have both learned to call these experiences by the same name?

On another tack, colour is also a word that is sometimes used about people. Everyone is coloured, in the sense that all skins have a colour, but 'white' people tend to call everyone with a different skin hue 'coloured'. Any more than cursory look will show that white people aren't really white, black people aren't really black and so on. Nevertheless, skin colours do vary. Under what circumstances is it relevant or polite to talk about the colour of someone's skin, or to call them 'coloured'?

Discussion plan: Colours

The following questions are designed to encourage your students to think about the concept of colour from the perspective of their own experiences.

1. Do you have a favourite colour? Why did you choose that particular colour?
2. How many colours can you see around you right now?
3. What is the most colourful object in the whole world?
4. Does everything in the world have a colour? (Could there be something that had no colour at all?)
5. Are your thoughts and dreams in colour?
6. If the answer to question 5 is 'no', does that mean that your thoughts and dreams are in black and white?
7. Can you imagine what the world would be like if there were no colours at all?
8. When you look at a blue ball, how do you know it is blue?
9. When you and your friend look at the same blue ball, how do you know that you are both seeing the same colour?
10. Is it all right to talk about people having colour?

Activity: Experimenting with colours

Ask your students to draw or colour in something using a particular colour — blue, say. Now ask them to draw over the top of the blue in a different colour — red, say. Now ask them what happened to the blue. Did it go away? What happened to the red?

As a (messy) variation, get them to mix different coloured paints or liquids together and talk about the results.

Next, shine different coloured lights (using coloured light bulbs or coloured transparent plastic) onto a particular object. Ask students 'If the colour of the light changes, does that mean that the colour of the *object* changes too?'

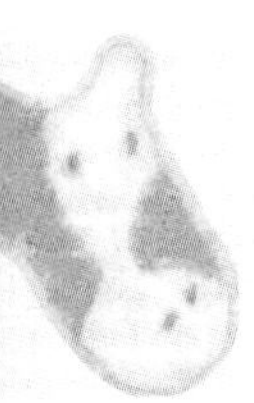

Finally, take your students outside (preferably on a sunny day). Ask them to look carefully at the colours around them — the grass and sky, for example. Ask them to imagine what would happen if the sun were a different colour (but make sure they do not look directly at the sun!). Would the grass and the sky have a different colour (as in the previous experiment)? At night, when the moon is out and the sun has gone down, do they think that the grass and the sky have *changed* their colour?

Leading idea 3: Thinking about measurement

The second black and white cow is thinking about questions like 'Why is the sun round?' and 'How can it be measured?'. Taken in one way, these questions might seem like scientific or empirical (i.e. factual) questions that could be answered readily enough by someone who knows enough astronomy. On the other hand, they also reflect some conceptual puzzles about the way things appear vis-a-vis the way they 'really' are. The sun might appear to be no larger than a small coin, but we know that it really is much, much larger (don't we?). So how can we be so sure that the sun is really round? Maybe it is really a cone or cylinder, and just appears round, because of the direction we look at it from? And even if it is round, it isn't really a circle but rather a sphere.

To a certain extent, issues relating to measurement, perspective and scale are factual: according to the best scientific knowledge available, the sun has a specific shape and size, and is a certain distance from the Earth. But to declare something to be a 'fact' might be to downplay or even ignore the child's own perception and experience. In so far as they need to know certain astronomical 'facts', they also deserve the chance to explore the differences and connections between such data and their own (subjective) perceptions. These links make genuine understanding — as opposed to the thought-less memorisation of bits of information — possible.

Discussion plan: Appearing and measuring

1. Why do you think that the second cow was thinking about (questions to do with) the sun?
2. How do you measure someone's height or weight? How about age? Do we measure that as well? How?
3. Do you have to have a ruler if you are going to measure something?
4. How do you measure a line? Is there only one right answer?
5. How do you measure a point or a dot? Is there only one right answer?
6. When something is a long way away — like the sun — how do you think we could measure it?
7. Does everything look small when it is a long way away?
8. If things look bigger or smaller when they are nearer or further away, how do we know how big they *really* are?

Exercise: Appearing round and being round

A sphere looks round no matter what angle you look at it from. Many other objects look round only from certain angles. Interestingly, we interpret as being round pictures and images which, strictly speaking, are not round. For example, a picture of a wheel seen from an angle is really an ellipse, but we see it as round. Young children's drawings generally do not recognise this — wheels are always drawn as circles. This exercise is designed to lead children to think about shapes, and the way we see them, a little more closely. Gather a number of round objects, and drawings of round objects. Some examples of round objects are balls (spherical e.g. tennis, soccer, billiard; oval e.g. football), a compact disc, a toilet roll, a Smartie, a spiral, a glass, a cone-shaped candle, a drink can, a pear. Among the drawings, include some that show obviously round objects, such as wheels, from front-on and oblique angles. It would probably be useful to have a plain drawing of an ellipse, as shown below.

Show your students the objects and drawings, asking them if they are round as you do so. Start with spheres and circles, then show them the other objects and drawings. In the discussion, explore the idea that objects can be round from one view but not from others. You can eventually ask the children whether the sun is round like a ball or round like a disc or cylinder. How do they know?

Activity: What can we measure?

Invite students, in groups of three to five, to measure some familiar objects: the length of a pencil, the size of their desk or table, their own height, etc. Ask them to do this in two ways: with and without a ruler (or similar measuring device like a tape-measure). Ask them how they could more accurately guess the measurements when they do not have a ruler.

Now ask them to look out the window at some objects that are further away: a tree, a fence, a bird, a roof, even the sky. Once again, invite them to measure them in two ways: by guessing or estimating, and by using a ruler. But they have to do the measuring from where they are inside the classroom. Ask them if they think this is possible.

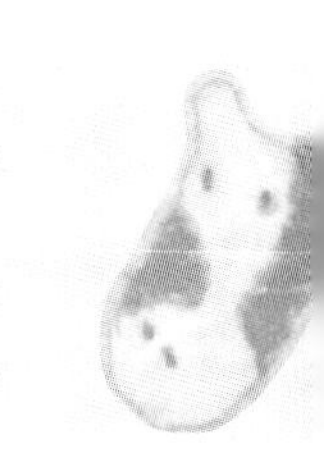

Ask them to examine the measuring device (ruler, etc.) itself. It is probably divided into units like centimetres and millimetres. Invite them to talk about how they could 'measure' the length of a centimetre. Would they have to use another ruler? Can they be absolutely certain that all centimetres have exactly the same length?

If you can find one, show your students an old-style ruler which measures things in terms of inches. Ask them if the two rulers produce different answers when they measure the same object.

Leading idea 4: Why do cows have four stomachs?

The next cow is thinking of her stomachs while chewing slowly. She wants to know why she has four stomachs, rather than five. This will probably surprise some children who are bound to ask why cows have more than one stomach (particularly those who think of their stomach as their 'insides', rather than a specific organ).

This leading idea can open up a discussion of why our bodies — and those of other animals — are the way that they are. Why do we have two eyes and two ears, but only one nose and one mouth? Are there any animals that are different in this regard? Does that mean that someone who is born with only one eye (or one eye that sees) is not human, or not normal?

The aim here is not to encourage children in the belief that such areas of scientific knowledge as anatomy are matters of guess-work or speculation, nor to come up with innovative ways to impart such knowledge. Rather, the point is to invite them to articulate, talk about and reflect upon the views that they do have about why things in nature are as they are. It is also to facilitate a better understanding of similarity/sameness on the one hand, and difference on the other.

Exercise: Would it make a difference?

In each of the following cases, say whether or not the change suggested would make a difference, and in what way.

	Would make a difference	Wouldn't make a difference	Not sure
1. Instead of one mouth, each person has two.			
2. Instead of two eyes, each person has four.			
3. Instead of two legs, each person has six.			
4. Instead of four legs, dogs and cats have two.			
5. Instead of one heart, each person has two.			
6. Instead of one head, each person has two.			
7. Instead of one body, each person has two or more (they keep the others in the cupboard at home and only use them on special occasions).			
8. Instead of one mind, each person has two.			

Activity: Counting things in nature

Divide students into small groups and invite each group to do some homework in order to find out what they can about (some) other animals and insects. For example, how many eyes do insects have? How many legs? How many heads? Does a cow really have four stomachs? Get them to draw some of these creatures, making sure they put in the right number of organs, limbs, etc.

Ask them to talk about why the world is full of such differences. Can they think of any reason at all why cows might need more than one stomach, or flies more than two eyes?

Activity: Aliens and monsters

Divide the class into pairs. Ask each pair to imagine an alien or monster that is very different from themselves, in terms of their physical appearance — and, in particular, the number of organs, limbs and so on. Invite each pair to draw (or describe) their creation.

Leading idea 5: What do cows think about?

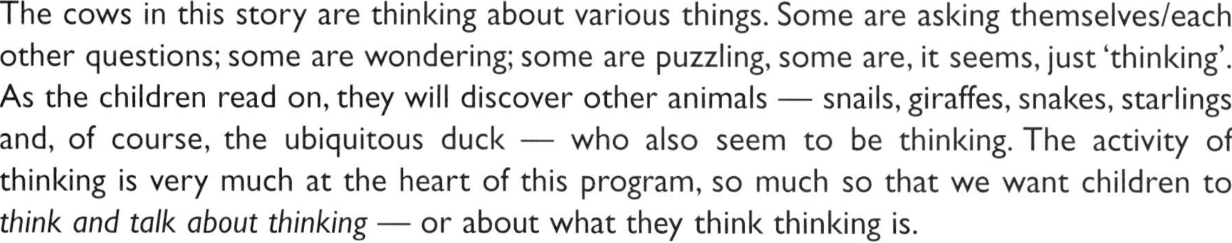

The cows in this story are thinking about various things. Some are asking themselves/each other questions; some are wondering; some are puzzling, some are, it seems, just 'thinking'. As the children read on, they will discover other animals — snails, giraffes, snakes, starlings and, of course, the ubiquitous duck — who also seem to be thinking. The activity of thinking is very much at the heart of this program, so much so that we want children to *think and talk about thinking* — or about what they think thinking is.

This leading idea suggests two ways in which children might think about thinking. The first way arises from the fact that — in these stories at least — non-human animals can and do think. This may be as unsurprising to young children as it is preposterous to (some) adults, but in any case, it provides an opportunity for children to think about some of the psychological connections and differences between themselves and other beings (not just other animals). Perhaps they will find that there are some things in the world which do not think at all, while there are others — like ourselves — who not only think, but think about thinking.

The second aspect of 'thinking' which emerges as a result of reading this story and its companions is that there appears to be more than one kind of thinking — or, more precisely, 'thinking' is a very general term for classifying or labelling many (but not all) of the things we do. Like the cows and other characters in these stories, we think in many ways: we wonder and we puzzle, we worry and hope, we decide and conclude, we imagine and we dream, and on and on. In fact, there are many words we use to describe the many and various mental activities and processes in which we engage. Some of these terms may not be familiar to young children (which is not to say that they do not think in these ways, merely that they are either unaware of their thinking, or unable to articulate it). On the other hand, many of the words we use to describe mental activity are familiar to — albeit not necessarily well understood by — children. Encouraging them to think about some of these is one way of opening up for them the power and richness of their own minds.

The topic of 'thinking' is very complex and crosses a number of different disciplines (philosophy, psychology, physics, medicine, language, literature). Even different philosophical traditions offer quite different theories and interpretations. In formally introducing this topic to young children, we should not be too ambitious. It would be more than sufficient for them to begin to understand and articulate some of the ways in which we do think. This, in itself, is no easy matter, notwithstanding the paradoxical fact that we really do not have to look much further than within ourselves!

You may want to come back to this topic and some of the exercises below at different stages of this program. [See also *Path* 1, *Field* 6]

Exercise: What do cows think about?

Do you think cows think about the following things? Don't forget to give a reason for your answer.

1. their babies (calves)
2. the grass that they eat
3. the people who milk them
4. their lives
5. their thoughts
6. their dreams

Exercise: Who thinks?

For each of the following, say whether you think that he/she/it thinks.

1. your pet
2. a fly on the wall
3. a tree
4. a baby that is one day old
5. an alien
6. a computer
7. your best friend
8. the whole world

Now go back over your answers and talk about how you could know. For example, if you think that your pet thinks, is there any way of being certain, or even checking?

Exercise: Is this thinking?

Say whether or not each of the following definitely is a kind of thinking, may be/is partly a kind of thinking, or definitely is not a kind of thinking.

	Is thinking	May be/ is partly thinking	Is not thinking	Not sure
1. wondering about the sun and the moon				
2. imagining that you are eating a chocolate ice-cream that is taller than you are				
3. having a scary dream				
4. watching television or looking at a picture book				
5. going for a walk				
6. eating a sandwich				
7. playing with your friends				
8. drawing a picture				
9. listening to your teacher talking				
10. feeling excited about something				

Leading idea 6: Being conscious

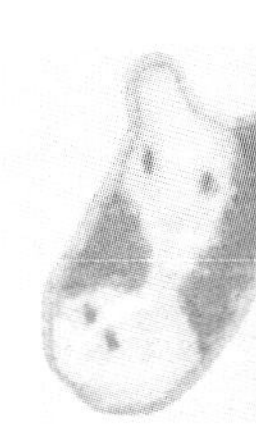

In a field, another black and white cow was *conscious* of her markings. You could begin discussion of this leading idea by asking your students what they think this means. Perhaps some of them have heard the term 'unconscious' (particularly in the context of a statement like 'He was knocked unconscious'). One tempting thought is to say that this pair of terms is similar to (or even the same as) the terms 'awake' and 'asleep', but are they? Perhaps a better simile for 'conscious' is 'aware'.

Although these terms might be hard for some children to grasp, they do reflect something about human beings which is important in the context of this program; namely, the idea that good thinking depends on our capacity to be *aware of ourselves*. Here consciousness is more than just a state of being awake; it is an awareness that we are alive and can think, wonder, imagine, dream, etc.

To return to the trigger for this discussion, does it make sense to suppose that a cow might be *conscious* of something? Rather than trying to persuade children that this is impossible because only humans can be conscious of anything, it would be preferable to allow them to speculate on what the world might be like if it contained cows (and other creatures) who were, in some sense, conscious.

Discussion plan: Conscious

1. If the cow was conscious of her markings, does that mean she could see her markings?
2. If the cow was conscious of her markings, does that mean she could think about her markings?
3. If the cow was conscious of her markings, does that mean she had a picture of them in her mind?
4. Are pets like dogs and cats conscious? What are they conscious of?
5. Are you conscious right now?
6. Are you conscious when you are asleep?
7. Could a flower be conscious?
8. Could a rock be conscious?
9. Is it better for you to be conscious or unconscious?
10. Would it be better for an ant to be conscious or unconscious?

Exercise: Being conscious

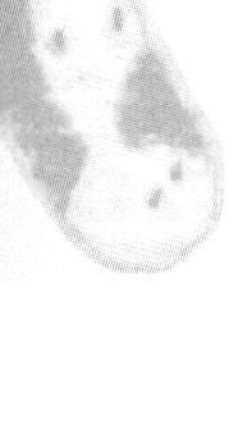

Which of the following things are you conscious of?

1. your nose
2. your heart beating
3. your hands
4. your feelings at the moment
5. your thoughts

Which of them can you make yourself 'not conscious' of?

Leading idea 7: What's the use of it?

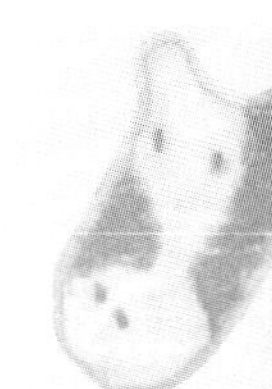

'What's the use of being mottled like this rather than having horizontal stripes?', another cow wondered. For many people — especially those in contemporary western societies — questions about usefulness have become extremely important (some might say, *too* important in so far as they direct our attention away from the intrinsic value of things). Yet it is also true that for young children, questions to do with usefulness may not be uppermost in their thinking. Typically, they do not evaluate their enjoyment of a game or activity by considering as extrinsic a criterion as 'use'. If they find something interesting or wonderful, that is enough for them.

On the other hand, children can be very demanding when they confront something which they do not understand. Sometimes this demand translates into a question about use ('But what's it for?'), but it is, perhaps, more accurate to say that what drives children's sense of wonder is a desire to make sense of things, rather than a need to know how they might be used.

In discussing the concepts of use and usefulness with children, we need to remember that the adult concern with utility, efficiency, etc., may be more a part of our agenda than theirs.

Exercise: What use is it?

For each of the following, say whether or not it has a use. If you think it does have a use, say what that use is; if you think it does not have a use, would we better off without it?

	Has a use	Doesn't have a use	Not sure
1. the whiskers on a cat			
2. the hair on your head			
3. your eyebrows			
4. brown skin rather than white or yellow skin			
5. four fingers and a thumb rather than five fingers			
6. class rules			
7. younger brothers and sisters			
8. your dreams			
9. music			
10. school			

Leading idea 8: Doing things together

A duck who happens to be passing by helps the last cow answer her question about the usefulness of her markings. The duck brings all four cows together and then realises that these cows were born to be … geography teachers!

It seems that we can discover something about the cows when they are brought together; something that we could not have known when they are separate. We can go further and suggest that what we discover is *not even true* when the cows are separate. It only becomes true when they are brought together.

Underlying this particular illustration are several ideas that are worth exploring with children. One is that when a collection of objects (or parts of an object) is considered as a whole, we can sometimes perceive or discover features of the whole that we were unaware of previously (this is one aspect of part-whole relationships). Another idea is that when people and things work together, they can (often) achieve more than when they work independently or separately. [See also *Tree* 2, 6]

Exercise: Doing things together

Say whether you think that the following do things better when they are separate or when they are together. In each case, give an example to explain your answer.

	Better when they are separate	Better when they are together	Not sure
1. cows eating grass in a field			
2. ants			
3. drops of water			
4. letters of the alphabet			
5. players in your favourite football team			
6. pieces in a jigsaw puzzle			
7. babies			
8. children			
9. grown-ups			
10. heads (minds)			

Activity: Apart and together

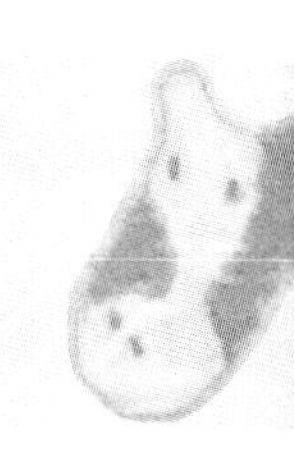

Divide the class into groups of about four or five. Explain that you want each group to do/make up something, such as a drawing, a small play, or a story. Each member of the group has to contribute something — one part of a drawing, one particular character or action, or a few lines (or even just a few words) of a story. Each person should work out his/her own particular part and then put them together in the group. Invite each group to present their creation to the whole class.

Leading idea 9: Being born to do something

Another idea which emerges here is that of 'being born to be (or to do) something'. This is reminiscent of a philosophical thesis known as *fatalism* which says that 'Whatever will be, will be', or 'Things will happen in a certain way regardless of what we do or what we think — the future is out of our control'. Fatalism, in turn, is connected to the concept of *freedom* — or, rather, to the denial of freedom. If fatalism is true, then how can we be free to determine the course of our own lives and action?

When trying to encourage your students to think about (some of) these ideas, it goes without saying that we must not stray too far from those things which are part of their normal experience. *Fate* may not fit into this category, although *freedom* is a more plausible candidate. Moreover, it is reasonable to ask them if they think that people (and perhaps things) are born (or made) in order to do certain specific things, such as be a mother or father, have a certain kind of job as an adult, be used in a certain way (as a table, as a chair), etc. As long as the discussion remains connected to the realm of children's experiences and conceptual understandings, it can urge them to extend their thinking beyond the immediacy of the 'here and now', to issues about what happens with the passing of time.

Exercise: Being born to do something

For each of the following, say whether you think that it was born, made, neither or both.

	Was born		Was made		Neither		Both	
1. a baby								
2. an adult								
3. a mountain								
4. a book (like the one you are reading/looking at now)								
5. a poem or nursery rhyme								
6. a story								
7. a cow								
8. a number (like 2 or 7)								
9. a word								
10. the whole world								

Now consider the same list again. This time talk about whether each thing was born or made to be, or to do, *something* (and, if so, what?).

Leading idea 10: Philosophy

The duck concludes that the cows should 'leave [the] philosophy to one side for the moment'. Apart from the use of a metaphorical expression that some children may not be familiar with, there is the unspoken assumption here that the cows have been doing philosophy. Here is another chance to focus on one of the moves that are part of good thinking — in this case, identifying assumptions. It is also an opportunity to talk with your students about what they think philosophy might be. Of course, if the word 'philosophy' is completely new to them, they might not have too many thoughts about this. But experience suggests that even quite young children have a sense of what philosophy is, and so stand to benefit from talking and thinking about this issue.

Once again, this topic is one to which you might want to refer at various points during the program. [See also *Tree* 6]

Discussion plan: What is philosophy?

1. Does the duck in the story assume that the cows were doing philosophy?
2. Were the cows in the story doing philosophy?
3. Is philosophy about answering questions?
4. Do you think philosophy is about asking questions?
5. Can you do philosophy by yourself or only with other people?
6. Do you think you could do philosophy without actually saying anything?
7. Do you think it is possible for children to do philosophy?
8. Is it a good idea to do philosophy? Why/why not?
9. What do you think philosophy is?

on a path

On a path a snail thought about arms and legs and wings. It tried to imagine how it would feel to fly. It contemplated its shell and wondered why it was spiral and not square. «What kind of noise would I make if I had a voice?» It wondered if its trail would be useful for finding its way home... An observant duck who just happened to be passing overhead realised that the snail didnt need arms, legs, wings or a voice because it had found its own perfect form of expression. On a path a snail thought about arms and legs and wings. It tried to imagine how it would feel to fly. It contemplated its shell and wondered why it was spiral and not square. «What kind of noise would I make if I had a voice?» It wondered if its trail would be useful for finding its way home... An observant duck who just happened to be passing overhead realised that the snail didnt need arms, legs, wings or a voice because it had found its own perfect form of expression. On a path a snail thought about arms and legs and wings. It tried to imagine how it would feel to fly. It contemplated its shell and wondered why it was spiral and not square. «What kind of noise would I make if I had a voice?» It wondered if its trail would be useful for finding its way home... An observant duck who just happened to be passing overhead realised that the snail didnt need arms, legs, wings or a voice because it had found its own perfect form of expression. On a path a snail thought about arms and legs and wings. It tried to imagine how it would feel to fly. It contemplated its shell and wondered why it was spiral and not square. «What kind of noise would I make if I had a voice?» It wondered if its trail would be useful for finding its way home...An observant duck who just happened to be passing overhead realised that the snail didnt need arms, legs, wings or a voice because it had found its own perfect form of expression. On a path a snail thought about arms and legs and wings. It tried to imagine how it would feel to fly. It contemplated its shell and wondered why it was spiral and not square. «What kind of noise would I make if I had a voice?» It wondered if its trail would be useful for finding its way home... An observant duck who just happened to be passing overhead realised that the snail didnt need arms, legs, wings or a voice because it had found its own perfect form of expression. On a path a snail thought about arms and legs and wings. It tried to imagine how it would feel to fly. It contemplated its shell and wondered why it was spiral and not square. «What kind of noise would I make if I had a voice?» It wondered if its trail would be useful for finding its way home... An observant duck who just happened to be passing overhead realised that the snail didnt need arms, legs, wings or a voice because it had found its own perfect form of expression. On a path a snail thought about arms and legs and wings. It tried to imagine how it would feel to fly. It contemplated its shell and wondered why it was spiral and not square. «What kind of noise would I make if I had a voice?» It wondered if its trail would be useful for finding its way home... An

Leading idea 1: Thinking and imagining

The opening lines of this story pick up the crucial idea of 'thinking' (see leading idea 5 in *Field* above: you might want to take your students through some of the exercises that appear there). A snail was *thinking* about arms and legs and wings. And it tried to *imagine* how it would feel to fly. As with the cow in the first story, there is a puzzle over whether snails really can think, and if so, what they think about. But it seems that the more we think about it, the more puzzling the whole 'activity' of thinking itself looks! What kind of activity is it? Is it something we do with our minds (or brains) like we do certain kinds of physical activities with our hands and bodies?

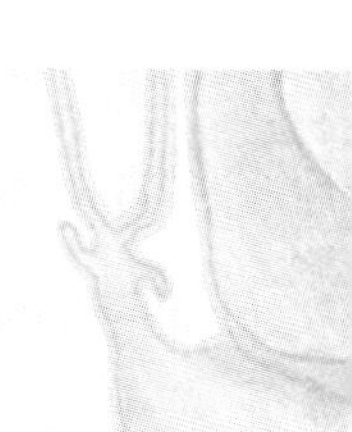

If thinking is an activity — that is, something we *do* — does it have an object (that which is thought about) or not? This question calls to mind the familiar grammatical distinction between *transitive* and *intransitive* verbs. Transitive verbs, like 'eating', 'hitting' and 'throwing', have an *object*, whereas intransitive verbs, like 'swimming', 'jumping' and 'breathing', do not (or do not always). If I eat, then there must be something which I eat: this is the *object* of the activity of eating. I can't just eat, without eating something. On the other hand, if I swim, there may not be any thing which is the object of that activity. Still, I am always swimming *in* something (a pool, the ocean) and (usually) swimming in order to get somewhere (even if it is just to the other end of the pool).

So our question now becomes 'Is thinking (and also imagining, wondering, hoping, puzzling, believing …) transitive or not? (Is it like eating, or is it more like swimming?) In other words, when I am thinking, is there always something which is the object of my thinking: that which I am thinking of or about? Alternatively (or, perhaps, in addition), do I always think *in* something and does my thinking always have a goal or a purpose?

It is tempting to follow the grammar of our language, and say that when I am thinking of my pet cat, then the object of my thinking is my cat. Just like when the snail thought about arms and legs and wings, we see these objects pictured in the story, suggesting that these are the things that the snail is thinking about.

But this is very problematic, as can be seen with an example like 'I am thinking about (or imagining) a nine-headed dragon'. What if there is no such thing (as is often the case when we imagine)? How can it be there for me to think about? Someone might say, 'Well, the dragon, which is the object of your thought, is just in your mind, or your imagination'. The following activities are designed to stimulate discussion over this kind of issue.

Discussion plan: What happens when we think and imagine?

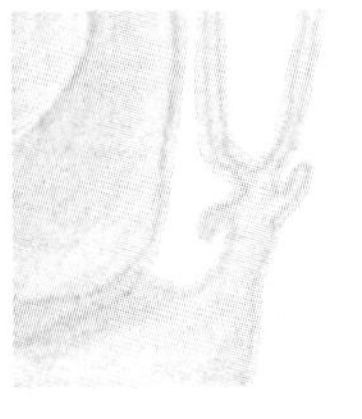

1. How can a snail think about arms and legs and wings?
2. When you think about your arm, do you see your arm?
3. Now close your eyes and think about your arm. Do you see your arm? Where is it?
4. Imagine that your arm is so heavy that you can't lift it. What are you seeing now?
5. Think about being really cold. Do you feel cold when you do that? Do you have a cold thought?
6. Think about being really happy. Do you feel happy when you think about that? Can you make yourself happy just by thinking about it?
7. Imagine that you can fly like a bird. Do you have a picture of yourself flying? When you imagine this, does it feel like you are flying?
8. Are there any things that you just can't think about, no matter how hard you try?
9. Think about your bed at home. Is there a real bed that you are thinking about?
10. Think about a nine-headed dragon. Is there a real nine-headed dragon that you are thinking about?

Exercise: Imagining something really weird

Try to imagine what it would be like to be the following (share your ideas with the whole class):

1. your best friend
2. a snail on a garden path
3. a monster from outer space
4. a computer
5. a thought

Imagine what it would be like if snails could fly and birds had to crawl around in the garden. Do you think that the snails and the birds would like this idea?

Leading idea 2: Shapes

The snail contemplated its shell and wondered why it was spiral and not square. Shape is a fascinating concept — especially to young children for whom the discovery of how things look and feel is central to their ongoing exploration of the world about them. Yet, as we found with another perceptual or 'sensual' concept — that of colour — when we dig a little deeper, we begin to uncover some complex questions and issues. In fact, exactly parallel questions can be asked here (see *Field* 2): What exactly are shapes? Is a shape like *square* something which is inside a square-shaped object like a cube? Or are shapes not really *in* things at all? But if they are not, then where, if anywhere, are they? In the mind, perhaps? Would that mean that our thoughts have a certain shape?

Discussion plan: Shapes

The following questions are designed to encourage your students to think about the concept of shape from the perspective of their own experiences.

1. Do you have a favourite shape? Is it a square, or a circle, or maybe a spiral like the shape of the snail? Why did you choose that particular shape as your favourite?
2. Do you think that the snail knows what shape it is?
3. How many shapes can you see around you right now?
4. Does everything in the world have a shape? (Could there be something, even in your wildest imagination, that had no shape at all?)
5. Do your thoughts and dreams have a shape?
6. When you look at a circle, how do you know it is a circle?
7. When you and your friend look at the same circle, how do you know that you are both seeing the same shape?

Exercise: Imagining shapes

If the following things had a shape, what do you think it would be?

1. the colour red
2. the colour black
3. the colour white

4. the sound of a fire-alarm (or the school bell)
5. your favourite song
6. a really awful smell
7. the taste of honey
8. a head-ache
9. feeling sad
10. feeling happy

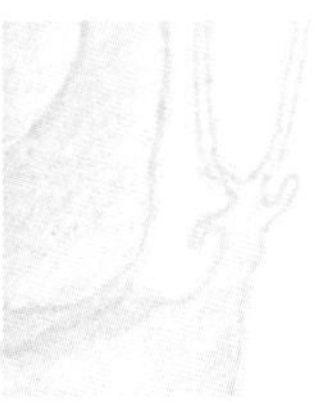

Leading idea 3: She and he

Your students may wonder about the picture on page 5 of *On a Path*. Does it contain two snails joined together, or one snail with two heads? And what about all those strange symbols that look a bit like raindrops made from arrows and crosses?

Some of the children might recognise these symbols as conventional designators of 'female' and 'male'. In this context, the puzzle about how many snails are represented here raises some questions about 'snail gender' that you might like to explore with them. Are there boy snails and girl snails? Is a snail a he or a she? Could a snail be both a he and a she? How is this possible? Is there something special about snails which is not true of (most) other creatures? This might also be an opportunity for older students to do some research.

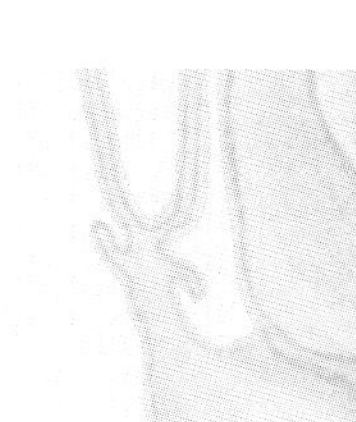

How about people? Is everyone either male or female? Could someone be both, or neither? And what is the difference between male and female anyway? How important is it that you know if someone is a male or a female? Does it make a difference to how you interact with them? Such questions provide an opportunity to invite children to reflect on some topical questions regarding the basis of gender distinctions.

In some languages (interestingly, not English) and cultures, literally every thing that can be described or named (from God, to people, to tables and chairs and feelings) has a gender: it is either male or female.

Some of these questions may be regarded as too sensitive for classroom discussion. But to deny children the opportunity to deliberate over the concepts and experiences which give shape to their lives would seem unreasonably restrictive, to say the least. The plain fact is that children are confronted with gender issues every day of their lives, often from sources which have powerful vested interests.

It can be argued that the very sensitivity and complexity of gender-related topics renders them ideal candidates as topics of inquiry — so long as we remember that our primary objective here is to help children think well about matters of importance, and not to impose, indoctrinate or manipulate.

Exercise: Girls and boys

Talk together about some of the animals and plants that you know about. Can all living things be divided into 'male' and 'female'? Do you think that the snail in the picture could be both? Does this mean that we should not refer to snails as 'he' or 'she', but simply 'it'?

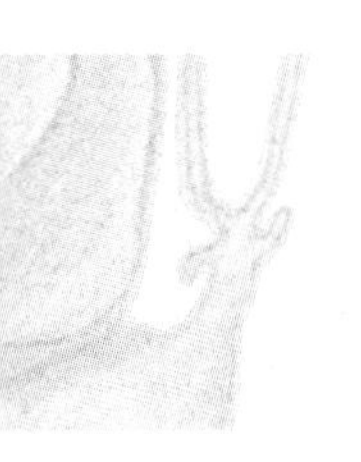

How about insects, or plants? Do they divide into male and female or not? How could we tell? And how about things that we make or build — like tables and chairs, and computers? Can these be divided into boys and girls or not?

If you are a boy, try to imagine what it would be like to be a girl — and *vice versa*. Would you still be the same person you are now? Imagine you met someone and you couldn't tell if they were a boy or a girl. What difference would it make?

Leading idea 4: If I had a voice ...

'What kind of noise would I make if I had a voice?' asks the snail? There is the hint of a *paradox* here — that is, a situation which seems, at first sight, to be impossible or self-contradictory. [See *Plain* 6 for a Discussion plan and an Activity on possibility.] Even if the snail just thinks about this question or asks it of her/him/itself, it seems to involve the use of language and, so, requires some kind of voice. And yet, the way the question is framed indicates that that the snail definitely does not have a voice!

It is worth noting that there is a connection between the idea of making a noise or a sound, and other experiences involving the senses. You might like to review the earlier discussions on *Colour* and *Shape*. (*Field* 2, *Path* 2).

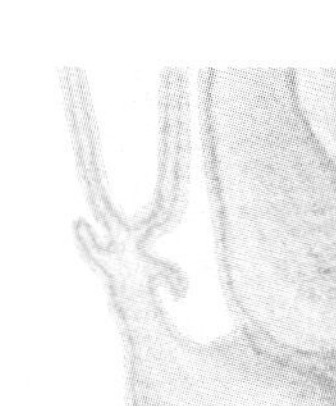

The snail's question is in the form of a *counterfactual*. It carries the implicit assumption that what follows the words 'If I had...' — in this case the idea of the snail having a voice — is not actually true (literally: it is counter to the facts). A counterfactual question or statement invites us to imagine what things would be like in circumstances which are not actually true. Examining counterfactuals can serve as a stimulus for better thinking in a number of ways: for example, exercising our *imaginations*, and identifying the *consequences* of acting or behaving in a certain way.

Although counterfactual statements are relatively easy to make, working out whether a particular counterfactual statement is true or false (or somewhere in between, like 'reasonable' or 'possible') is another matter. Helping children think about what would, or might, make such a statement true, is an important aspect of their developing understading of truth and reasonableness.

Discussion plan: Making a noise and having a voice

1. Where do you think your voice comes from?
2. What kinds of noises can you make without using your voice?
3. Could you still talk [say anything] if you did not have a voice?
4. Does a snail make a noise?
5. Does a snail have a voice?

Exercise: What would it sound like?

Try to imagine what the following would sound like if they had a voice or could make a noise.

1. a caterpillar
2. a dragon
3. your doll or your teddy bear
4. a mountain
5. the air
6. the colour red
7. a stomach ache
8. a very happy feeling

Exercise: If I had ...?

This exercise is designed to help your students become more comfortable with the use of counterfactual statements and, more generally, with the idea that even though certain things *are not true*, we can imagine how things would be *if they were true*. Whether or not they learn to use the word 'counterfactual', the idea of saying something true (or plausible) that involves some kind of projection *beyond* what is actually true, is very important when it comes to developing an awareness of what truth means.

Ask students to complete the following and encourage discussion about whether the resulting sentence is really true (or, at least, plausible).

1. If I had two mouths, then I could ...
2. If I had two heads, then I could ...
3. If a snail could talk, it would say ...
4. If I was 100 years old, I could ...
5. If I didn't have to go to school ...
6. If I was older than my parents, then ...
7. If every day was Saturday, then ...
8. If no one told the truth, then ...

Leading idea 5: Signs and symbols

A *sign* is a marker or indicator — a shorthand way of informing people about something (which street you are in, for example), or directing them to do something (stop at a red light, for example). You could ask your students to find specific examples of signs in these stories (bearing in mind that in a sense, every word and picture *signifies* — that is, is a sign of — something). Is the snail's trail a sign? If so, what is it a sign of? How about the spiral shape of the snail's shell, or the markings on the cows? Are they signs? How could we decide?

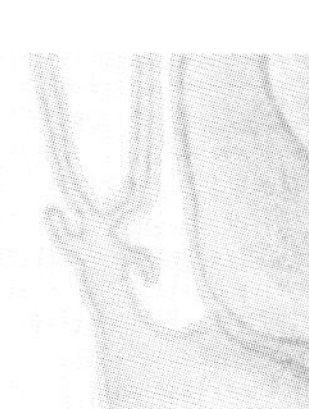

A *symbol*, on the other hand, has a more complex purpose. It represents something, but not in an obvious or clear way as a sign does. The Australian flag represents (that is, symbolises) Australia, its people, its government, its history. As such, it has an emotional significance that a sign does not usually have (it can also be quite contentious, in so far as it gives rise to positive emotions in some people, but negative emotions in others). The Sydney Opera House has become a national symbol, as has Uluru (or Ayers Rock) although where the former symbolises a technological achievement, the latter represents an affinity with nature. Even the names we use for things can be symbolic: the changing of the name from 'Ayers Rock' to 'Uluru' was highly symbolic of the increasing recognition of Australia's aboriginal past.

Our behaviour is often symbolic too. Shaking hands with someone or wearing our best clothes to mark a special occasion can be regarded as symbolic actions. [This discussion has drawn on Matthew Lipman's *Philosophical Inquiry,* p. 228.]

Visual signs and symbols. There is a vocabulary of visual signs and symbols just as much as there is a vocabulary of words. Unlike words, however, visual signs can vary quite a lot without losing their meaning: they have more flexibility. In our present society, which is highly visually-oriented, children need to become literate in pictures just as much as in words.

Of course, there are many different types of visual signs and symbols that we can recognise. The most obvious are those that are highly stylised and widely used to convey information, either straightforwardly as a sign (e.g. the drawings used on road signs), or in more complex ways as symbols (e.g. those used by commercial operations). Children can usually read a lot of these before they can read words, and their recognition is a step on the way to reading. Commercial operators, of course, play on this in advertising for small children, who can recognise (say) the golden arches long before they could read the word McDonald's. Advertisements are designed to pack a great deal of meaning into the symbol (e.g. fun, tasty food, being cool).

In part, learning to draw means becoming fluent in the production and use of visual signs and symbols. Given the saturation of our world with visual images, children will build up a stock of representations by looking around them, and by seeing how others in their environment (peers, parents, teachers) produce and use them. Learning through social situations is as important for visual literacy as it is for verbal literacy.

It is interesting to see how people from different cultures use quite different signs for similar objects. Although the globalisation of culture makes it increasingly difficult to find people who are totally unfamiliar with our western symbolic representations, there are well documented studies of how people from other cultures have not been able to read symbols varying from such obviously stylised and culture bound representations as maps (which take a lot of learning even within our culture), through to such seemingly simple and obvious signs as arrows to point out directions.

Signs and symbols are important tools for communicating, explaining and representing and, as such, are valuable topics for your students to think about.

Activity: Visual signs

Ask your students to look at the following drawings and tell you what they are. How much do they look like the real thing? For example, does the house look anything like their own house? If not, how did they know it was a house, then? As a follow up, ask your students to draw simple signs for some very common things (either give them a list of things — dog, bell, tree, car, kite, flower, moon, sun, bed and so on — or ask them to think up their own).

Activity: Pictorial signs we know

In each of the books, the illustrators have used stylised signs for everyday objects. Ask the students to go through the books and find the drawings that are used to get across the following ideas:

1. fence
2. leg
3. cities
4. sun
5. male
6. direction finding
7. aeroplane
8. thought
9. female
10. trees
11. hand
12. ruler
13. wing
14. bird

Exercise: Identifying signs and symbols

This activity is designed to stimulate discussion and reflection about the meaning and use that signs and symbols have in our lives.

Bring into the classroom a number of items (or pictures/photos of items) and ask your students to decide if they are signs, symbols or, perhaps, both. If it is not practical to bring the objects in, then bring a picture or photo, or else show students what you are talking about. Here are some of the objects you can use.

1. a wedding ring
2. the name of your school
3. a card or label with each person's name on it
4. an Australian folk song like 'Waltzing Matilda'
5. a traditional Aboriginal or ethnic song
6. the hands of a clock
7. clapping after a good performance
8. the label on a can of soft drink
9. a smiling face
10. a police officer's cap or helmet

Leading idea 6: Home

The snail wondered if its trail would be useful for finding its way home. You could begin a discussion of the concept of home by asking your students what they think of this notion. After all, if the snail carries its home on its back, doesn't it follow that it is *always* home? If not, then does it even make sense to talk about a snail having a home?

These questions can lead to a more general consideration of the concept of (a) home. While it should not be assumed that every child has a home, it is reasonable to assume that this concept is one which is important to them. For some, home is a physical place: the one in which they live with other members of their family. Even here, the physical concept is complicated by such realities as divided families — concerning which children may declare that they have two different homes.

For others, the idea of home has more emotional than physical significance. Home is that place (whatever it is) where they feel comfortable, relaxed, secure ('at home', as we say). Ideally and often in practice, these two aspects overlap: we feel 'at home' when we are (physically) at home, but this may not be the case for everyone. It would be interesting for children to reflect on the idea of home, not just from their own perspective, but from that of other people, other cultures, other living things.

Discussion plan: Home

1. Does a snail have a home? If so, where is it? If not, where does it live?
2. Do insects and spiders have a home? If so, where?; if not, where do they live?
3. Do wild animals, like lions and tigers, have a home? If so, where?; if not, where do they live?
4. Where do trees live? Would they call that place 'home'?
5. If a bird's nest is in a tree, does that mean that the tree is the bird's home?
6. Do wind and rain have a home?
7. Is it possible for a person to have more than one home?
8. Could someone say that their school or classroom is their home?
9. Can you think of something or someone that doesn't have a home?
10. Do you think that everything in the world needs a home?

Exercise: Imagine that you live ...

What would it be like to live in the following places?

1. in a country where no one spoke your language
2. in a tree-house
3. in a cupboard
4. in a small room with six other people
5. on the street
6. under the sea
7. on the moon
8. inside a giant soap bubble

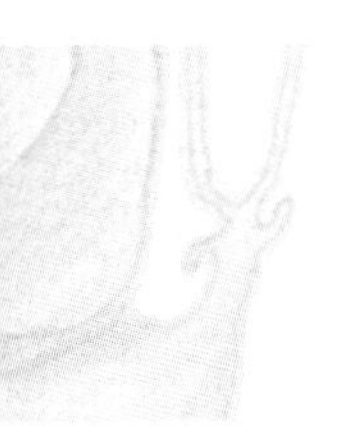

Activity: Drawing a home

Think about a make-believe animal like a monster or dragon. Now think about what kind of home it would live in and draw a picture of that animal at home.

Leading idea 7: Talking to others and talking to yourself

[*Note*: Leading ideas 7 to 10 are provoked by a single sentence in the story — the final sentence, in fact: 'An observant duck who just happened to be passing overhead *realised* that the snail didn't *need* arms, legs, wings or a voice *because* it had found its own perfect *form of expression* ...']

As your students read through these stories, they will notice that the characters do quite a lot of thinking. There are cows which *ruminate* and *ponder*, ducks that *realise* and *resolve* things, a snail that *imagines*, *contemplates* and *wonders*, a giraffe that *speculates* and *decides*, and so on. [See also *Field* 5, 6; *Path* 1]

One view of thinking is that it is just like talking, except that we do it quietly rather than out loud. In other words, thinking is a way of 'talking to oneself'. This view may seem rather narrow: after all, some of our thoughts take the form of pictures or images and are not so much 'spoken' as 'seen' or even 'felt'. Nevertheless, most children will relate to the idea of talking to themselves and will enjoy the chance to discuss the role of this activity in their lives.

It's worth noting here that just as thinking might, in some cases, be regarded as talking to oneself, so talking can sometimes be regarded as 'thinking out loud'. Indeed, we could say that when children engage in dialogue within a community of inquiry, they are, in a literal sense, 'thinking together'. [See also *Plain* 5]

Activity: Different types of thinking

Read one or more of the books to the children. As you read, ask the children to stop you every time you read a word that describes one of the animals thinking. Collect the words on a board or sheet of butcher's paper. Can the children add any more words for types of thinking?

Discussion plan: Talking and thinking

1. When you are with your friends, who does (most of) the talking?
2. When you are with your friends, who does (most of) the listening?
3. Can two people talk at the same time and still listen to each other?
4. Do you ever talk to yourself? If you do, who listens?
5. Do you ever think out loud? How do you do that?
6. Can you talk to your friend just by thinking (that is, without saying anything out loud)?
7. What is the difference between talking to yourself and talking to another person?
8. What is the difference between talking to yourself and thinking?
9. Could you still talk if you never, ever, thought about anything?
10. Could you still think about things if you never, ever, talked to anybody?

Activity: Making up a story

Divide the children into pairs. Ask each member, in turn, to make up a story just by thinking about it (it doesn't have to be very long), and then tell it to the other person. The story can be about anything at all.

Exercise: Thinking out loud

Which, if any, of the following 'activities' can only be done silently/in your mind and which can only be done out loud?

	Can only be done silently	Can only be done out loud	Both	Not sure
1. yelling				
2. talking				
3. going for a walk				
4. giggling				
5. laughing				
6. wondering about what you will be when you grow up				
7. telling a story				
8. imagining that you can fly like a bird				

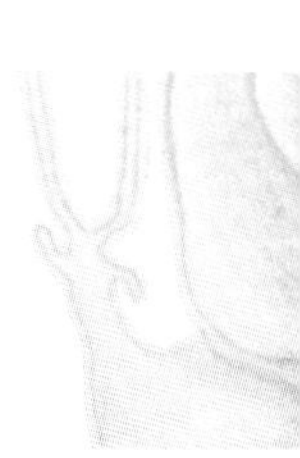

Leading idea 8: Needing and wanting

The duck who was passing overhead realised that the snail did not *need* arms, legs, wings or a voice. Perhaps the snail *thought* that it needed these things, perhaps it *wanted* them, but it did not need them. To *need* something is to require something that is necessary or desirable — normally, in order to fulfil some further need, interest or desire. For example, I need air in order to breathe and stay alive, you need to go to bed early so that you will be fresh for school tomorrow, etc. You may or may not want to go to school tomorrow, and even if you do, you may or may not want to go to bed early. But assuming that you need to go to school (presumably in order to fulfil some still further need), you also need to go bed early.

To *want* something, on the other hand (in the familiar sense of the term), is to desire or like something so much that you wish to have it. Where what we need has a fairly clear *objective* basis — that is, needs extend beyond what we feel, like or desire at a particular time — what we want is much more *subjective* — it depends mainly on our feelings and attitudes. I may want an ice-cream even though it might be hard to justify the claim that I need it; on the other hand, I may need to go to bed early even though I may not want to. Children want all sorts of things (or, rather, they claim to want them which, arguably, is the same thing), and they may say that they need them, but it does not follow that they really do need them. Conversely, they need things which they do not always want (or, at least, they claim not to want).

Over and above the distinction between needing and wanting — a distinction which, itself, is not always clear-cut — some questions remain. Are the things that we need always good for us? In what circumstances is it okay to obtain or receive something which we want but do not need? Which is ultimately more important: satisfying our needs or satisfying our 'wants'?

Given this familiar tension between what we need and what we want, the potential for conflict — particularly inter-generational conflict — is evident. Helping children become clear about the distinction in question, and allowing them to reflect, together, on a range of problematic cases may be one way of preparing them to deal, constructively, with the worst elements of this conflict. It may also assist them to formulate a more considered understanding of what they judge to be important in life.

Discussion plan: Needing and wanting

1. Do you think that the snail wanted arms and legs?
2. Do you think that the snail needed arms and legs?
3. Do you think that the snail wanted wings?
4. Do you think that the snail needed wings?
5. Can you think of three things that you really want?
6. Can you think of three things that you really need?
7. Can you think of something which you want but don't need?
8. Can you think of something which you need but don't want?
9. Can you think of something which you need and want?
10. Can you think of something which you don't need and don't want?

Exercise: Needing or wanting?

For each of the following, indicate if it is appropriate to say that you need it, want it, both, or neither.

	Need it	Want it	Both	Neither
1. rain				
2. sunshine				
3. vegetables				
4. chocolate cake				
5. holidays				
6. school				
7. teachers				
8. money				
9. trees				
10. lots of friends				
11. school rules				
12. a good imagination				

Leading idea 9: 'Why' and 'because'

The passing duck realised that the snail didn't need arms, legs, wings or voice *because* it had found its own perfect form of expression. The word 'because' is very important here; it signals that the duck is giving a *reason* — in other words, explaining why the snail did not need these things.

Learning to ask, and answer, '*why*' questions is crucial to good thinking in several respects. For one thing, it enables us to *understand* or *make sense* of things that would otherwise be unclear or confusing. Finding out why you suddenly jumped up and ran out of the room, for example (because you felt sick), helps me to make a connection that, in turn, leads to a better understanding of your behaviour. Further, the giving of reasons is an important part of trying to *justify* what people say and do. Feeling sick might be judged as a good reason for running out of the room, whereas feeling bored might not be (in the context of accepted social conventions which, of course, might themselves be called into question and, hence, supported by reasons).

Consider a slightly different example, concerning a statement rather than action. If someone says that the level of immigration into Australia should be reduced, we would be entitled (indeed, obliged) to ask 'why', that is, to ask for a reason. And once again, we would be looking to see if the reason(s) given not only helps to make better sense of the original claim, but also provides some kind of justification or warrant for it. In this case, a good reason would serve to support the *truth* of the claim — or, at least, to make it seem *reasonable*.

What makes a reason a good reason? This might be a good question to discuss with your students, although it may be one which they cannot really respond to until they have had a lot of experience in asking for and giving reasons. Among the criteria that might be suggested as to what constitutes a good reason are the following: good reasons have to be factually correct; good reasons have to be relevant to the situation or statement at hand; good reasons help us to understand what was said or done; and good reasons are known by, or familiar to, the person who is asking for the reason in the first place [*Philosophical Inquiry*, p.253]. In any case, it is worth encouraging your students not only to ask for and provide reasons for their views, but to talk about whether or not these reasons are good ones.

Using words like 'why' and 'because' to signal that reasons are being asked for and provided, is a useful way to introduce children to the logical structure of language and thinking. Given that young children may not be particularly interested in exploring logical connections as such, we do not have to say much more than this here.

However, it is worth pointing out that the signpost words 'why' and 'because' do not always refer to a request for reasons. Often, we ask 'why' when we want to find out *how something works*. In such cases, our 'why' question is rather similar to a 'how' question, and can be understood as a request for an explanation in terms of *causes and effects*. If someone asks me 'Why do you have a toothache?', I could give a reason in terms of cause and effect: 'The toothache is the result of certain nerve endings being affected by decay ... ' etc. Even though it answers the 'why' question, it has more to do with cause and effect than with reasons. Certainly, there is no attempt here to justify anything: the toothache happens because it is a bodily response to other physical events.

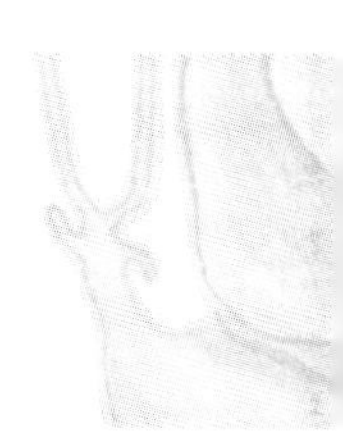

Some philosophers have argued that causes *are* reasons (or, alternatively, that reasons are causes). While this debate need not concern us, it can be noted that one and the same event can be accounted for or explained by both a reason *and* a cause. Consider my toothache again. An alternative response to the 'why' question might have been 'I have a toothache because I was greedy'. This answer does not conflict with the one given above. Rather it provides a reason for why I acted foolishly (e.g. by eating a whole bag of chocolates), instead of a cause which offers a physical explanation of my toothache. Notice that in this case, it might not make much sense to ask if the reason given is a good one — unless this is just another way of asking if eating the chocolates really did *cause* the pain. However, it would be quite appropriate to ask whether being greedy is a good reason for why I ate all those chocolates.

One more point worth noting. Part of the skill in requesting and giving reasons is learning when it is not necessary or appropriate to look for reasons. Children often answer 'why' questions with comments like 'I just do, that's why' and such a response may be fitting in certain situations. Can we, for example, expect that matters of personal taste be justified or supported by reasons? (Of course, this leads to the question of what constitutes a matter of personal taste!) Perhaps expressions of love or friendship fall into this category.

One of the aims of discussing the activity of asking for and giving reasons is to help raise students' awareness of just this issue: specifically, when is it permissible to defend an opinion by saying something like 'Well, that's just my opinion and I don't have to give a reason'? [See *Tree* 5, 7 for more on reasons]

Activity: Finding reasons

Read through the stories again and this time ask students to pay particular attention to situations when reasons are being asked for and/or given. Help them to see the value of using words like 'why' and 'because' as signposts to reasoning.

As a second step, in those cases where they are able to identify a request for reasons, talk with them about whether the response offered constitutes a good reason; if so, then why, and if not, then why not. If a request for reasons is not answered in the story, invite students to come up with their own reasons.

Exercise: Is this a good reason?

For each of the following, choose the statement(s) — if any — which you think provide(s) a good reason for the opinion given. Of course, you should be prepared to give a reason for your choice.

A *Opinion*: I think it will rain today.

Statements:

1. It rained yesterday.
2. It hasn't rained for weeks and we really need it.
3. The weather forecast said it would rain today.
4. There are thick dark clouds in the sky.

B *Opinion:* I'm not going to have any dessert tonight.

Statements:
1. Last time I ate dessert, I felt sick.
2. I'm not that hungry.
3. I don't like sweet food.
4. I want to rush back to watch television.

C *Opinion*: Going to school is really important.

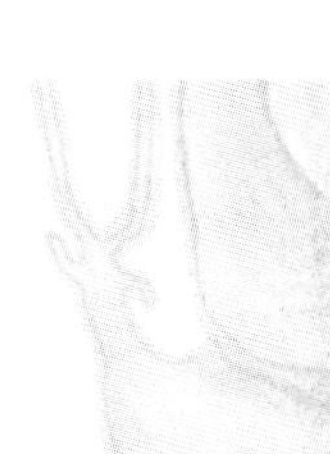

Statements:
1. If we didn't go to school, we would get bored.
2. School is a good place for making friends and having fun.
3. School is where you learn things that matter.
4. Everyone says that going to school is important, so it must be.

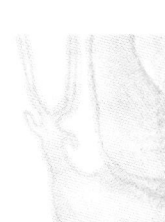

Exercise: Should we ask for a reason?

For each of the following statements or actions, say whether or not it is important to ask for a reason. .

	Isn't important to ask for a reason	Is important to ask for a reason
1. *Lee*: I like smooth peanut butter, but I can't stand crunchy peanut butter.		
2. *Liz:* I love Nickolai but I hate Robert.		
3. *Juan*: Boys are better than girls.		
4. *Tamara*: I like wearing red clothes, but I can't explain why.		
5. *Chen*: I think that people who are born in another country shouldn't be allowed to live in Australia.		
6. *Talya*: I think that anyone who wants to live in Australia should be allowed to.		
7. *Kim*: I just know that there are aliens out there somewhere.		
8. *Christa*: My doll is prettier than yours.		

Leading idea 10: Forms of expression and perfection

The snail had found its own perfect form of expression. But what does this mean? What is a *form of expression*? What makes a form of expression (or, indeed, anything) *perfect*? And how could a simple snail *find* such a thing?

Some children might see a connection between these questions and *Path* 7. They might say that the beautiful trail made by the snail is the closest that the snail can come to actually *thinking*. The trail is a silent record of the snail's behaviour, just like thinking is a silent record of the things that we humans do and say. These children are perceiving an analogy between thinking and the snail's activity of leaving a trail.

Other children might say that the trail is nothing other than a series of marks made by the snail. The snail doesn't mean to leave a trail, and the trail itself does not tell us anything about what is going on inside the snail.

There are several complex issues here and it would be unreasonable to expect that your students could unravel all of them. It would be quite an achievement if they could talk together about the phrase 'form of expression' — given that it occurs on the final page of the story — and give some sense to it from the perspective of their own experience and reflection. The exercises which follow are designed to help them in this task.

Discussion plan: The snail's form of expression

1. Does every snail make a trail?
2. Does every snail make the same trail?
3. Does the snail make a trail on purpose?
4. Does the snail's trail mean something? If so, what?
5. Is the snail trying to express something by leaving a trail? What might that be?
6. Could the snail express itself in some other way? How?
7. Do you think that snails can talk?
8. Do you think that snails can think?

Exercise: Forms of expression

For each of the following, talk about whether it has a form of expression and, if so, what that form of expression is (or might be). Feel free to use your imaginations here!

1. a lion
2. a butterfly
3. a caterpillar
4. a duck
5. a giraffe
6. an egg
7. a dead cat
8. a rose
9. a cactus plant
10. the earth
11. a star
12. you

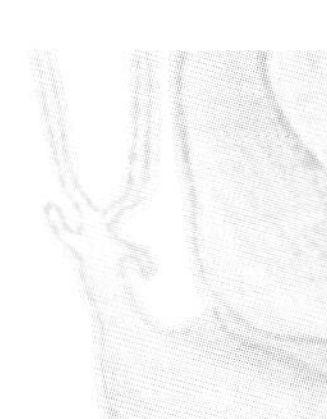

Activity: A perfect object

Draw the following:

1. a snail and a perfect snail
2. a cloud and a perfect cloud
3. a circle and a perfect circle
4. a person and a perfect person

On a plain

On a plain a giraffe was feeling a little bored with its surroundings. It tried imagining that the sky was the sea, but the view was still very horizontal. It wondered «Maybe living very close to the ground is more interesting.» But seeing things from an ant's point of view made its neck hurt. «Perhaps it's fun to be a snake,» it speculated, but realised that its tongue wasn't the right shape for saying 'hiss'. So it decided to just eat and dream of other places. A travelling duck flying over the plain was surprised to see that it had almost reached its destination... But discovered that apparences and imaginative giraffes can be deceptive. On a plain a giraffe was feeling a little bored with its surroundings. It tried imagining that the sky was the sea, but the view was still very horizontal. It wondered «Maybe living very close to the ground is more interesting.» But seeing things from an ant's point of view made its neck hurt. «Perhaps it's fun to be a snake,» it speculated, but realised that its tongue wasn't the right shape for saying 'hiss'. So it decided to just eat and dream of other places. A travelling duck flying over the plain was surprised to see that it had almost reached its destination... But discovered that apparences and imaginative giraffes can be deceptive. On a plain a giraffe was feeling a little bored with its surroundings. It tried imagining that the sky was the sea, but the view was still very horizontal. It wondered «Maybe living very close to the ground is more interesting.» But seeing things from an ant's point of view made its neck hurt. «Perhaps it's fun to be a snake,» it speculated, but realised that its tongue wasn't the right shape for saying 'hiss'. So it decided to just eat and dream of other places. A travelling duck flying over the plain was surprised to see that it had almost reached its destination... But discovered that apparences and imaginative giraffes can be deceptive. On a plain a giraffe was feeling a little bored with its surroundings. It tried imagining that the sky was the sea, but the view was still very horizontal. It wondered «Maybe living very close to the ground is more interesting.» But seeing things from an ant's point of view made its neck hurt. «Perhaps it's fun to be a snake,» it speculated, but realised that its tongue wasn't the right shape for saying 'hiss'. So it decided to just eat and dream of other places. A travelling duck flying over the plain was surprised to see that it had almost reached its destination... But discovered that apparences and imaginative giraffes can be deceptive. On a plain a giraffe was feeling a little bored with its surroundings. It tried imagining that the sky was the sea, but the view was still very horizontal. It wondered «Maybe living very close to the ground is more interesting.» But seeing things from an ant's point of view made its neck hurt. «Perhaps it's fun to be a snake,» it speculated, but realised that its tongue wasn't the right shape for saying 'hiss'. So it decided to just eat and dream of other places.A travel-

Leading idea 1: Being bored

The giraffe feels a little bored with its surroundings. It's not unusual for children to say that they are bored, or that something is boring. These two ways of putting it point to an interesting property of the nest of concepts surrounding boredom: that they can be ascribed to people (who are bored) or to objects, events, other people and suchlike (which are boring). Indeed, it seems more plausible to claim that *boredom* is a relational property, which always involves a person and an object of boredom. So saying 'I am bored' is always a shorthand way for saying something like 'I am bored with this toy' or 'I am bored with having nothing to do'. Similarly, 'This show is boring' is a shorthand for 'I am bored by this show'.

But what sort of relationship is *boredom*? Some statements of a relationship always remain true, such as that fire is hotter than ice, due to the fact that they describe physical facts. Boredom, on the other hand, describes an attitude, and this attitude may be changed in a number of ways. It may be that we see the boring object in a different way, so the level of attention paid to the object is important. It may be that the bored individual changes their attitude — attitude is linked to mood, tiredness and many other factors. Some of these factors are under the control of the person involved, and they can make an effort to overcome boredom, as does the giraffe in the book. The giraffe tries to achieve this by changing itself — taking up the point of view of other creatures. Humans, on the other hand, will often react to boredom with their surroundings by changing the surroundings — shifting the furniture, redecorating and so on.

Furthermore, since attitudes depend on the interests of the person involved, what is boring to one individual may not be boring to another, or to the same individual at a later time, when their interests have changed (see also the next leading idea).

Helping children to explore these aspects of *boredom* can assist them to see that there is often a sense in which they choose to be bored, and could very well choose not to be. It will also assist them to see that the causes of boredom are different for different people, which may make them a little less disposed to get into arguments about whether, say, football or dolls really are boring. Children in early childhood need plenty of opportunities to build their growing awareness that their own view of the world is not shared by everyone, and practice in trying on the attitudes of others. [See also *Plain* 3]

Activity: Who finds these things boring?

Ask your students to draw (or, for older children, write) on a piece of paper one or more things or situations they find boring. Gather the class together in a circle. Ask a number of children to explain their choice of something boring, and to give a reason why they found it boring. Then ask if anybody disagrees. Why don't they find it boring?

Discussion plan: Getting over boredom

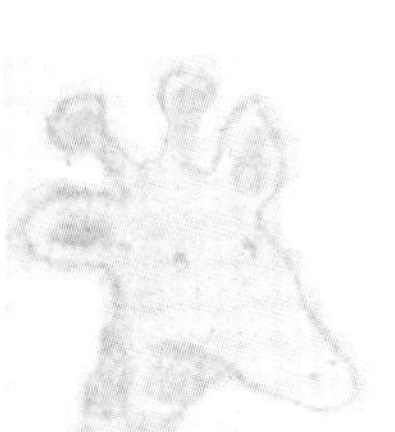

1. Why was the giraffe bored at the start of the book?
2. What did the giraffe do to try to overcome boredom? What worked?
3. When have you been bored? What did you do about it?
4. Have you ever been bored with something and then found that it wasn't boring after all? What changed your mind?
5. Are there any things that are always boring to you? Do you think that there are any things that are always boring to everyone? What? Why?
6. Are there any things that are never boring to you? Do you think that there are any things that are never boring to anyone? What? Why?
7. Are there some people who find almost everything boring? What sort of people are they?
8. Are there some people who find almost nothing boring? What sort of people are they?
9. If a person is bored by something, is it the person's fault or the thing's fault?

Activity: Boring things and attention

Gather together a variety of objects, some of which look immediately boring and some of which don't. Try to choose some which look boring but aren't. Here are a few suggestions — you can probably think of more:

- a jack-in-the-box painted in a dull colour
- a material that looks plain from a distance but has a fine, intricate pattern when looked at closely

→

- a colourful fan that folds away into a simple-looking, flat shape
- a cardboard pop-up book in a plain brown-paper cover
- a stone that looks dull when dry, but reveals hidden patterns when wet.

Hold up the objects one by one, without letting the children get too close a look at them, and ask the children to say whether they are boring or not boring. Put the 'not-boring' ones to one side and get some of the children to explore the 'boring' objects more closely. Which ones do they find are not boring after all? Why do they think so? From here, you might ask them whether something that looks boring might turn out not to be boring after all. If so, what makes the difference?

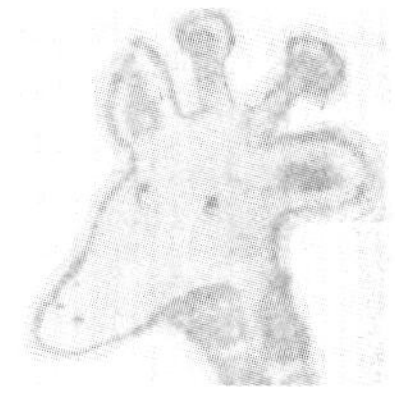

Leading idea 2: Interesting

Clearly, *interesting* is a companion concept to boring. Like boring, it relates a person to an object, via an attitude towards that object. It connects a person with certain interests to an object (situation, other person, etc.) that meets those interests in some way.

The word 'interests' is itself an interesting one. In one sense, our interests are those things that interest us. We are generally more or less aware of what things interest us. Although it can be the case that we find that we have become interested in something 'despite ourselves', so that we gradually recognise that we have an interest in it, adults at least have usually sorted out what their interests are. However, while young children certainly know when they are interested in some things, they can be much less clear about what exactly are all the things in which they are interested, or the particular aspects of the interesting experiences that are of interest to them. Part of growing up is discovering what it is that interests us, and teachers have a particular role to play in exposing children to plenty of experiences, both so that children can discover what interests them, and so that their interests can expand through exposure to new situations. These sorts of interests are interesting to us.

In another sense, our interests are those things that are good for us. It is not so clear that we know our own interests in this sense, though a modern liberal democracy assumes that all adults do. Children, however, are often treated as if they do not know what is in their interests. It is adults who take it upon themselves to do things 'in the interests of the child'. Important among these interests is the child's interest in getting an education, so that they can become able to represent their own interests. Teachers, like parents, often have to act in the child's interests, even contrary to the child's immediate wishes. Such actions are often called paternalistic. These types of interests may not be interesting to us at all (it is in our interests, for example, to take out the garbage, but it is probably not very interesting).

Discussion plan: Making the boring interesting

1. When the giraffe was bored, it tries to imagine that the sky was the sea. Is the sea more interesting than the sky? Why?
2. Do you think the giraffe would have been more interested in its surroundings if it lived in the mountains rather than on a flat plain? Why?

3. Do you think that living very close to the ground is more interesting than being high up in the air like a giraffe?
4. The giraffe tries to make things more interesting by looking at them differently. Do you think changing the way you look at things makes them more interesting?
5. If you were the giraffe, how would you make your surroundings more interesting?
6. If you find something boring, do you think it is better to change the thing, or to change yourself? Why? How could you change yourself?

Activity: What makes it interesting?

Collect together some pictures from magazines of people engaged in a variety of activities — engaged in different pastimes, playing various sports, reading, doing household chores, involved in various jobs, sitting and thinking and so on. Scatter them around the classroom and ask your students to pick out a picture of an activity that interests them. Get one at a time to explain to the others in the group why it interests them. Try to probe for more detailed and specific answers than 'it's fun' or 'I like it'. Use the second 'why?', so that when they give an unfocused answer like the above, ask why they think it would be fun, or what about it they particularly like.

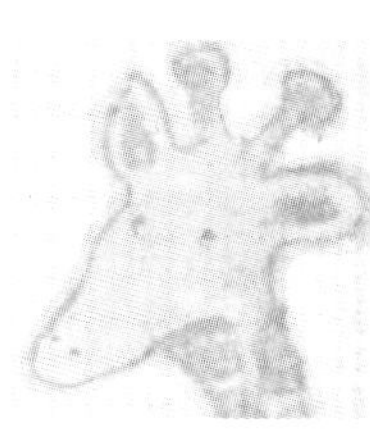

Exercise: Interesting and interests

Explain to the children that 'interest' can have two meanings: an interest of mine can be something I like to do, or it can be something that is good for me. Then ask them to say which sort of interest the following are. Each one might start a discussion about our interests.

	Interest = Good to do	Interest = Good for me
1. playing with my toys		
2. eating up all the food on my plate		
3. eating lots of sugary sweets		
4. watching television		
5. going to bed on time		
6. reading books		
7. talking to my friends		
8. going to school		
9. thinking about what I want to be		
10. thinking about words like 'interest'		

Leading idea 3: Trying out different ways of being

Many stories for young children have characters who want to be different from what they are, and this story is like that in some ways. *On a path* has a similar theme. However, the giraffe is somewhat different from many of these characters for, rather than wanting to become something else, it seems merely to be trying out their way of life as a means to break the boredom of the plain.

Trying out different roles is something that children often do. Many of their games are 'make-believe' and involve becoming, for a while, someone or something quite different. It is a practice that is extremely important in their development, because it helps them to understand the points of view of others (see the next leading idea). Such empathy is vital in a number of ways, not least because it is an essential element in becoming a more moral person. Studies indicate that adolescents who get into trouble with the law often have low levels of empathy with others.

Child developmental psychologists Jean Piaget and Lawrence Kohlberg have argued that the child starts life completely egocentric, and that becoming able to decentre, or see things from another perspective, is an essential developmental step. More recent work shows that children seem to have a natural empathetic reaction from a very early age, possibly right from birth. Nevertheless, both schools of thought on this matter agree that imaginative play is a vital part of refining the ability to see things from another's point of view (see further discussion under the next leading idea).

Accordingly, it is, as teachers know, important to give children many opportunities to imaginatively explore different roles. Further, we think that it is also important for them to think about what is happening when they enter into role play. Taking on another role is not becoming someone else. First, the giraffe does not take on all the characteristics of the ants, only some of them — the closeness to the ground — and then, only with its head. It slithers like a snake only with its neck. Indeed, it realises that it cannot take on all the snake's characteristics, because its tongue is the wrong shape. Even more than the physical characteristics, it is hard to see how the giraffe can possibly take on the thoughts and beliefs a snake might have (assuming a snake can be said to have beliefs, or even thoughts).

Discussion plan: Being, and pretending to be, an animal

1. Why does the giraffe want live close to the ground?
2. Why does the giraffe want to be a snake?
3. Do you think that the giraffe could be a snake?
4. If the giraffe has its head close to the ground, how different is it from when it has its head in the air?
5. If the giraffe could say 'hiss', would it still be a giraffe?
6. If the giraffe could slither on the ground as well, would it still be a giraffe?
7. If the giraffe lost its legs as well, would it still be a giraffe?
8. Can a giraffe think snaky thoughts?
9. Can you pretend to be a snake? While you are pretending to be a snake, in what ways are you like a snake? In what ways are you still you?
10. Would a snake be able to think in words, or would it think in some other way? What would snaky thoughts be like?

Activity: Being an animal

Ask for a volunteer who then has to pick an animal to be. As the child takes on the role of their animal, get the other members of the group to tell you the ways in which the child is like the animal they have chosen. You can also ask for suggestions from the audience as to how the child could be more like their animal.

Possible extension: Get the children to evaluate whether the suggestions are achievable or not. For example, a girl may be acting out being a tiger. A suggestion to bare her teeth would be feasible, whereas a suggestion to grow a stripey tail would not.

Alternative (for older children): Ask your students to form groups of two or three. Each child can take a turn at choosing their animal, while the others make the list of similarities and suggestions for improvements. The child in role can do the evaluation.

Discussion plan: How others see us

In each book, the duck comes along at the end and sees things a little differently to the other animals in the book. In general, others do see us somewhat differently from the way we see ourselves. This can be very helpful to us at times, particularly if we are prepared to listen to them. Young children are often having things pointed out to them by others, frequently adults.

1. What does the duck do at the end of each of the books?
2. Why can the duck tell each animal something they can't see for themselves?
3. Can you remember a time when someone saw what you were doing differently from the way you saw it?
4. Did it help you, or did it hinder you?

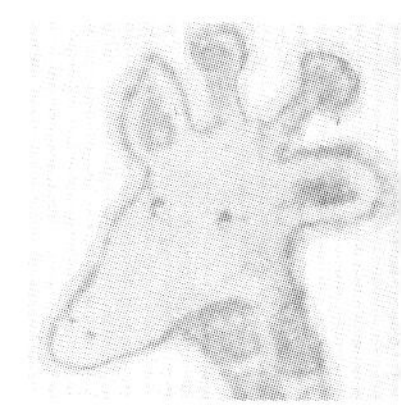

Leading idea 4: Points of view

We often talk about someone's point of view. This is a spatial metaphor: literally, a person's point of view is the place from which they see things — the place where their eyes are. In the story, this is the surface meaning of the line on page 4 where the giraffe tries to 'see things from an ant's point of view'. Getting its eyes down to the ant's level makes the giraffe's neck hurt.

Metaphorically, the term 'point of view' has a much wider meaning. I do not see things from your point of view if I move my eyes to the place where yours are. Instead I have to take on your beliefs and interests, at least hypothetically. Such an empathetic understanding of another is very difficult for children and not too easy for many adults.

So when children pretend to be a different person or different animal, they are restricted in their ability to become that person or animal by the way they are in themselves. To be empathetic with someone else can be just to imagine what you would do if you were in their position, with the interests and beliefs that you have. So the giraffe, for instance, might think that to be a hungry ant would mean trying to climb trees to get leaves to eat, because a giraffe would want leaves when it is hungry. Although children can never fully become someone or something else, their imaginative play, and later their attempts to empathise with others, will become more authentic if they are able to hypothetically take on, for the moment, the interests and beliefs they think the other holds. It is even better if they take the trouble to find out what those interests and beliefs are.

Discussion plan: Points of view

1. Would the giraffe be different if it could only ever see things from close to the ground? In what ways?
2. Would the giraffe's point of view be the same as an ant's if it always lived close to the ground?
3. Would your point of view be the same as an ant's if you always kept your head close to the ground?
4. Would your point of view be the same as your teacher's if you sat in the teacher's chair?

5. Do you have to become somebody else so that you can understand their point of view?
6. What does 'point of view' mean?

Activity: Physical points of view

Remember the old story about the blind men describing the elephant. Each of them can touch only one part of the elephant, and so each has a quite different idea about what an elephant is. The one who feels the trunk thinks an elephant is like a snake, the one who feels a leg thinks it is like a tree and so on.

For this activity (which will need plenty of preparation!), find an object which will feel different if touched from different directions. Put it in a box, and cut several holes, just big enough for a hand to fit through, in the box. Cover the holes with cloth, so the children can't look in, but can put their hands through a slit in the cloth. Ask a few children to feel the object through different holes, describe what they feel and then guess what the object is. Eventually you can open the box and show the object to your students.

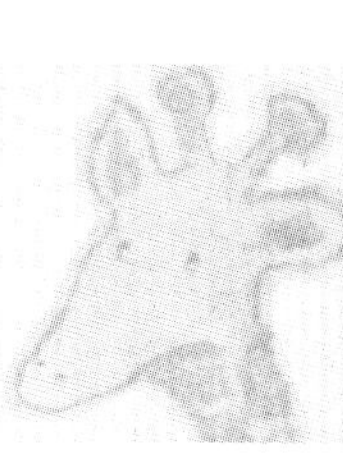

Variation: Collect some photographs of everyday objects photographed from unusual angles. Ask the children to work out what they are.

Leading idea 5: Internal dialogue

The giraffe talks to itself several times in the book as it grapples with the problem of overcoming its boredom. As we indicated in the Introduction, talking to oneself is very like thinking, and there is probably a connection between the two. In this discussion plan and exercise, you can encourage your students to investigate the connections between the two. [See also *Path* 7]

Discussion plan: Talking to yourself and thinking

1. When the giraffe wonders 'Maybe living very close to the ground is more interesting', is it thinking or talking to itself?
2. Why do you think the giraffe says, or thinks, this to itself?
3. Do you ever talk to yourself out loud? When? Why?
4. Do you ever talk to yourself silently? When? Why?
5. If you talk to yourself silently, do you ever answer yourself?
6. Is talking to yourself silently the same thing as thinking, or is it different?
7. Can you think without using words?

Activity: Do we think in words?

Ask the children to close their eyes and get comfortable. Now ask them to think about one of the things on the following list. When they have had a few moments to do so, ask them to think about it using only words. Can they do it? Now, ask them to think about it, without using words at all. Is it possible?

1. going home from school
2. the last birthday party you went to
3. eating an ice cream
4. being at home in bed, listening to the rain on the roof
5. talking to your friend
6. being in the kitchen when your favourite meal is being served out onto plates
7. listening to your favourite music
8. trying to work out what to say when the teacher asked you a question

Leading idea 6: Perhaps and possibly

Children love speculating about what is possible and what isn't. The giraffe speculates by saying 'Perhaps it's fun to be a snake'. Is it possible for a giraffe to be a snake? In make-believe perhaps it is, but not in real life.

There are a number of ways in which something might be possible. The possible might be quite likely: if we decide to do it (it is possible I could buy you an ice cream); if things turn out (it is possible Essendon will win the flag this year). The possible might be very unlikely: if technology advances (it is possible that one day we'll have walls that are television screens); if the laws of science turn out differently (it is possible that people will be able to travel through time).

We can see that the concept of *possibility* is quite complex. Where does a giraffe being a snake fit into this? It depends whether we consider the sentence literally or metaphorically.

The literal version Could a giraffe literally 'be a snake'? This depends on what we think makes a giraffe a giraffe and a snake a snake.

What are the defining features of a giraffe? Young children tend to classify animals (and many other things) by external features, so something will be a giraffe if it has long legs, a long neck, orange hide with black blotches and so on. Children who think in this way are likely to argue that the giraffe could become a snake, if it lost its legs, changed its colouration and so on.

Older children, on the other hand, usually believe that there is some internal 'essence' that determines what certain animals are. For these children, no matter what you do to the giraffe in terms of external changes, it would still be a giraffe — one that looks like a snake, but is not a snake. Although this position is commonly held by children older than nine (and many adults), whether it is adequate is still a contentious issue.

Susan Carey, in her book *Conceptual Change in Childhood*, quotes the results of a good deal of experimental evidence that, in most children, this change (for animals) takes place between the ages of five and nine. Carey claims that this is equivalent to saying that the younger children make no distinction between appearance and reality (if you look like a snake, then you are a snake — see also *Plain* 10). A shift from describing objects in terms of appearance to describing them in terms of definitions and category membership takes place in respect to other kinds of objects (apart from animals) as well, but this shift may occur at different ages, depending on exactly what kind we are talking about.

Some children may opt for neither external features nor internal essence: they may argue that a thing is what we agree to name it, so that if we choose to call it a giraffe, it is a giraffe, but if we choose to call it a snake, it is a snake. Thus a giraffe could become a snake if we chose to call it 'snake'. This sort of position is the one made famous by Humpty Dumpty's remark in *Alice in Wonderland* that a word means exactly what he wants it to mean.

The metaphorical version Of course, the giraffe may not mean 'to be a snake' literally. The question might be better put: 'What's it like to pretend to be a snake?' or 'What's it like to do some of the things snakes do?'. In this sense, it is quite possible for the giraffe to be a snake. Still, the question remains as to how far the giraffe has to be like a snake, before it makes sense to say 'The giraffe is a snake'. [See also *Plain* 3]

Exercise: Perhaps

Which word or phrase from the list on the right could you use to replace the word 'perhaps' in each of the following sentences?

Perhaps I'll have chicken for dinner tonight.	I hope that …
Perhaps I could have gone to the beach instead.	I am wondering whether …
Perhaps I'll win the lottery.	It isn't true, but it would be nice if …
Perhaps ice cream would be tastier.	It would explain things if …
Perhaps I'm catching a cold.	I might have decided that …
Perhaps Superman could clean up all the rubbish.	If I decide to, then …

Discussion plan: What's possible?

When the children give their answers to each of the following, ask them why they think it is possible or not possible. Keeping the above versions of possibility in mind might help in assisting your students to distinguish several different senses of *possible,* but we are not suggesting that you should attempt to distinguish them all. A word of caution too: children will often come up with amazingly ingenious ways in which any particular thing could be possible — even that a circle could be a square. Of course, this is great practice in creative thinking.

Is it possible that …

1. a bird could be a pet?
2. a shark could be a pet?
3. a plastic bowl could be a boat?
4. a giraffe could be a snake?
5. a lion could be an eagle?
6. a song could be a brick?
7. a circle could be a square?

Activity: That's impossible!

Get the children to stand spread out around the classroom. Ask them if it is possible for them to do each of the following. If they think it is possible, then they are to do it. If they think it is not possible, then they are to stand with their hands on their head. After each activity, ask some of those who have their hands on their heads why they think it is not possible to do what you said.

Is it possible to …

1. stand on one leg?
2. stand on no legs?
3. stand in the middle of the air?

→

4. wave goodbye to your mother?
5. put your foot behind your head?
6. habjaw your snurgle?
7. be a snake?
8. pretend to be a snake?
9. put your hands on your head?

The last instruction ought to lead to some fun when you ask someone why they believe it isn't possible to put their hands on their head. They have had two contradictory instructions, leading to a puzzle about what to do. Putting their hands on their heads is a way of saying that they can't put their hands on their heads. How will they resolve it?

Exercise: Wrong or silly?

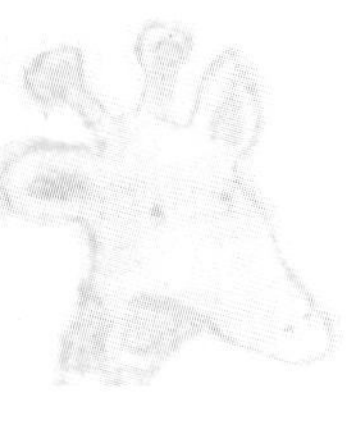

One of Susan Carey's research methods for finding out what sort of conceptual categories children used for organising their experience was to ask children to say whether they thought a sentence 'wrong' or 'silly'. Children will say a sentence is wrong if the attribution in it is one that could (logically) be true — that is, it would be possible in some situations, but not in ours. They say it is silly if they think that the attribution is impossible in any situation, because the property attributed could not possibly be applied to the object. To take an example from the book, if we say 'The giraffe was frightened', children are likely to say it was wrong. If, on the other hand, we say 'The rock was frightened', children are likely to judge that this is silly — rocks just aren't the type of thing that could possibly be frightened. Carey's main purpose was to determine what objects children thought were living, so she mixed animate and inanimate objects with properties that are attributable only to living, or to any, objects. Below, we have extended the range somewhat. Don't forget to ask children to give reasons for their answer, and to allow challenges from other children. You may well find the children might make a distinction between what is possible in reality and what is possible in fantasy.

Is it wrong or silly to say:

	Wrong	Silly	Both	Neither
1. The giraffe in the story was frightened.				
2. The rock was frightened.				
3. The fight was skinny.				
4. The weed was hungry.				
5. The air was solid.				
6. The thought was sleeping.				
8. The happiness was two metres tall.				
9. The discussion was breathing.				

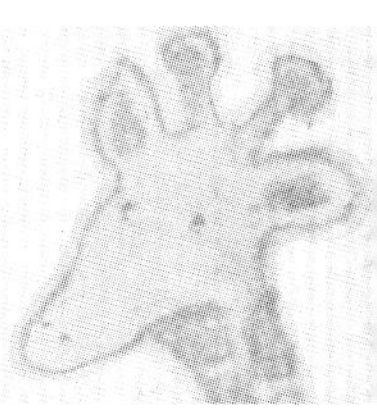

Leading idea 7: Fun

The giraffe wonders if it would be *fun* to be a snake. Children like to have fun. This is hardly surprising because we might be tempted to define 'fun' as things that you like doing. However, neither the Webster's nor the Oxford dictionaries mention liking or even pleasure in their definitions. The Oxford's first definition is concerned with hoaxes and tricks, while its second definition accords with Webster in mentioning play, recreation, sport and so on.

A little more thought might convince us that not everything we like doing is fun, either. Some things we like are more serious: and the phrase 'serious fun' has a certain oxymoronic ring to it. There is a certain flavour of playfulness that seems necessary to fun. And there seem to be other things that we like, which are neither serious nor fun. If I like eating cream puffs, it hardly seems to be a serious business, but we would hesitate to say that eating cream puffs is necessarily fun (although it can be, of course, if it has that element of playfulness about it).

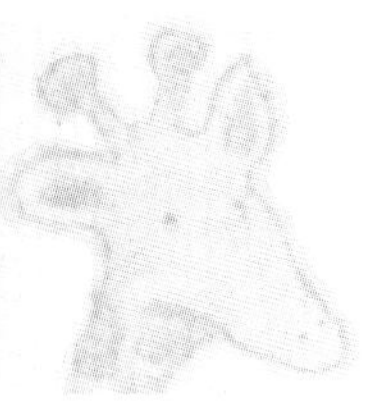

The reference in the Oxford dictionary to hoaxes and tricks reminds us that there is another word that is very close in form to fun: 'funny'. What is the relationship between these words? Is everything that is funny, fun? Is everything that is fun, funny? If something is funny to those watching, is it fun to those involved? Judging by television shows such as *Funniest Home Videos,* this is very doubtful. Does this mean that we ought not to find funny something that is not fun to those involved?

We have noted that dictionary definitions, while helpful, do not do the job of conceptual analysis for us. You will probably often find that when you ask 'What does X mean?', at least one of your students will suggest looking in a dictionary. To discover that a dictionary does not settle the question is an important philosophical discovery in itself: and 'meaning' is a central philosophical topic.

Apart from trying to pin down the central concept of 'fun' in your discussions, your students might also extend the investigation to consider such aspects as whether all people find the same things fun, or whether we can have fun at the expense of others.

Discussion plan: Fun

1. Why do you think that the giraffe thought it might be fun to be a snake?
2. Do you think it would be fun to be a snake?
3. Would it be fun to be a snake for the rest of your life?
4. Would it be fun to be a rock?
5. Is something fun if you like doing it? Can you give some examples?
6. Could you like doing something if it wasn't fun? Can you give some examples?
7. Could something serious be fun? Can you give some examples?
8. Could something fun be serious? Can you give some examples?

Exercise: Fun and funny

Ask your students to imagine the following situations. Would they be fun? Would they be funny? At the end, ask them: What is the difference between being fun and being funny?

	Fun	Funny	Not sure
1. You are at the swimming pool on a hot day, splashing water with your friends.			
2. You tell a joke to your friends and they all laugh at it.			
3. Somebody makes a joke about your new haircut and everyone laughs at you.			
4. You are watching a man walking along with a cake in his hands, when he slips over. The cake falls in the mud.			
5. You are walking along with your birthday cake in your hands and you slip over. The cake falls in the mud.			
6. You are watching a video of a girl your age swinging on a rope. The rope suddenly breaks. She falls down and hurts herself.			
7. You are swinging on a rope. The rope suddenly breaks. You fall down and hurt yourself.			

Activity: Fun things to do

Invite the children to think up something that is fun, and then to do it (you may want to put some restrictions on what they can choose). After they have been doing it for a few minutes, ask them to stop and get some of them to tell the class what they chose to do and why it was fun. Ask the rest of the class if they agree that the activity would be fun, and why or why not. If you pick some children who chose a particular narrow interest of theirs, then you are likely to get some interesting disagreement. You may well be able to draw out the connections here between fun and interest [See *Plain* 2].

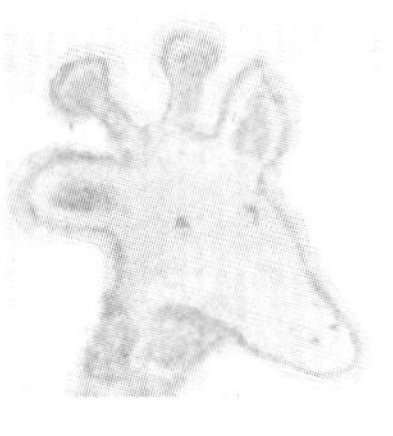

Leading idea 8: Dreaming

The giraffe decides to eat and dream of other places. Your students are likely to decide that it isn't possible to eat and dream at the same time, and it is likely that they will want to replace the word 'dream' with another word. What word? Daydream might be the most obvious one, which will lead to a consideration of what exactly the difference is between dreaming and related activities, such as daydreaming, wondering, imagining, wishing, letting your mind wander, seeing things, making up stories and so on.

Here are some of the criteria for distinguishing dreams from other similar activities that might be suggested:

1. whether it happens in the daytime or at night time
2. whether you can decide what to 'dream' about or not
3. whether your eyes are open or not
4. whether it makes sense or not
5. whether you are asleep or not.

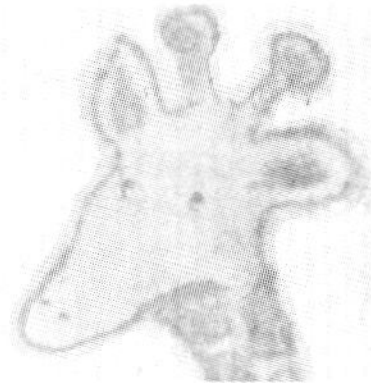

One word of caution here: when the discussion turns to dreaming, you are likely to find that the children will want to tell you all about the dreams they have had. This is likely to lead to a string of disconnected anecdotes — and this response is not confined to children, either. Humans seem to have a fascination with dreams and the stories of what happened in them. You may need to keep the discussion focused by asking those who recount their dreams how their story helps the inquiry into the difference between dreams and other similar activities.

Discussion plan: Dreaming

1. The giraffe decides to eat and dream of other places. Can *you* decide what you are going to dream about?
2. Could you dream and eat at the same time?
3. Do you think the giraffe was really dreaming? What else might it have been doing?
4. When you are dreaming, do you know you are dreaming?
5. What is the difference between dreaming and day dreaming/ wondering/ imagining/ wishing/ letting your mind wander/ seeing things/ making up stories?

Activity: Dreaming and related states

Tell the children you are going to ask them to sit very still and do some things. Here they are:

Tasks

1. Imagine that you are a butterfly.
2. Wish that you were a butterfly.
3. Daydream that you are a butterfly.
4. Dream that you are a butterfly.

After each task, ask a few of the class the following questions:

1. Was it easy to do what you were asked to do?
2. How did you do it? [*Or*, if it wasn't easy:] Why did you find it hard to do it?
3. What was it like?
4. [After the second and subsequent ones:] How does it differ from ... [an earlier task]?

Leading idea 9: Surprise

The duck was surprised to see that it had almost reached its destination. What is surprise? We are surprised when our expectations are not met. In order to be able to do things efficiently and effectively, we build up expectations of how things should be. The situation we find ourselves in gives us clues as to what will happen next. As we build up experience of the world, we become better at predicting the range of possible events that can follow. It is when these expectations are not met that we are surprised.

Young children are different from adults in two seemingly contradictory ways. First, because they lack experience, they have not built up a wide range of possible future outcomes of particular events. Hence, many things that we take for granted can surprise them. Gareth Matthews tells a delightful story (in *Philosophy and the Young Child*) of the four-year-old puzzled by the fact that he did not get smaller when he flew on a plane. After all, he had seen with his own eyes planes getting smaller as they ascended.

On the other hand, because their expectations have not had time to become deeply ingrained, things that surprise adults are often seen by many young children as unsurprising. Quite young children, for example, do not enjoy magic tricks (as opposed to the razz-ma-tazz that accompanies them) if they do not realise that the trick ought not to be possible.

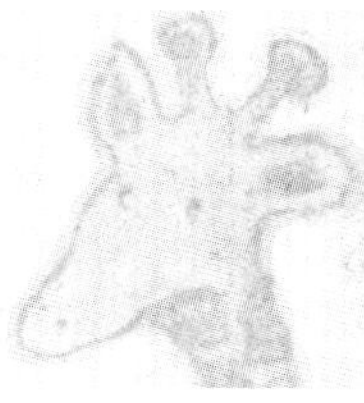

The concept of *surprise* is linked to puzzlement and wonder: key concepts in philosophy. If we were never surprised, it is doubtful that we would ever do philosophy at all. Out of a surprise, we can start to get interested in something new. This is why we suggest that you always start your philosophy discussions by asking what it is that the children themselves find puzzling or interesting.

Discussion plan: Surprise

1. Why was the duck surprised?
2. Would the duck have been surprised to find a city?
3. Would the duck have been surprised to find a giraffe pretending to be an ant?
4. Have you ever been surprised? What was it that surprised you?
5. Would you be surprised if your teacher came in with different coloured clothing on?

→

6. Would you be surprised if your teacher turned into a duck?
7. What makes something surprising?

Activity: Surprise endings

Ask for volunteers to do a mime. Each person has to mime some everyday action and then end the mime with a surprise. You can start the activity off with an example — say, mime that you are eating at a table with knife and fork and then mime picking up the fork with food on it and dropping it down the back of your neck inside your shirt. As each volunteer does their mime, ask the others to comment on what is happening. When the surprise comes, ask the others what made the new action so surprising.

A couple of suggestions here: many young children find it difficult to mime with enough accuracy and detail so that onlookers can identify what they are doing. If you use mime and role play in other activities in your classroom, this may not be true of your class. However, if you do run into this problem, you may need to have a few mimes up your sleeve to take over. Of course, practice in miming so others can recognise the activity is a good learning experience in itself, though it may require assistance from you.

Secondly, for many children, the surprise will be something like falling over or other mishap. Children seem to find mishaps to others endlessly amusing. In fact, judging by the perennial popularity of slapstick and shows like *Funniest Home Videos*, so do most of us (see also *Plain* 7: Fun). This suggests an alternative approach to this activity: show clips on video from such a show, and ask the children to explain why the clips are funny.

Leading idea 10: Appearance

The duck is misled by the appearance of the tree tops, since the giraffe has eaten them into a shape like a city. The tree tops appear to be a city skyline, but they aren't. The way things appear to be is the way they look to us. Sometimes, the appearance of something is no different from what it actually is but, if that is the case, we seldom talk about the way it appears to us, we just talk about how it looks.

Appearances can be misleading for many reasons: the light can be bad; someone might be trying to deceive us; we might not be paying proper attention. But one thing that seems to be central to most cases of being misled by appearances was referred to in the previous leading idea: expectation. We have a tendency to see what we are expecting to see, and not to see things that we don't expect to see. These expectations in some cases (like the first three optical illusions in the following activity) seem to be just 'built into' our perceptual systems, whereas others seem to be cultural, and others still due to individual knowledge and expectations.

The way things appear to be as opposed to *the way things really are* is an old philosophical topic. Our very earliest knowledge of philosophising comes from the writings about a group of Greeks from the 5th century BCE, known now as the pre-Socratics (because they were mainly active in the time just before Socrates). Their main philosophical concern was exactly this question of appearance and reality.

Discussion plan: Appearance

1. When the duck was flying, what did the shapes on the horizon appear to be to the duck?
2. What were they really?
3. Why do you think the duck saw something that wasn't there?
4. Can you think of a time when you thought something was one thing and it turned out to be another?
5. How did you find out that it wasn't the way it appeared to be?
6. Why are we sometimes wrong about what things are?

Activity: Optical illusions

The diagrams that follow are all well-known optical illusions. In each case, our visual systems (including the interpretation of images in our brains) gives us a wrong answer. We unconsciously make some assumptions which are generally helpful in interpreting such images, but which mislead us in these cases.

Diagram 1: Ask your students which of the upright lines is longer. Then measure them with a piece of paper laid against them. [In fact, both are the same length.]

Diagram 2: Ask whether the upright line or the horizontal line is longer. [Again, both are the same length.]

Diagram 3: Ask your students whether all three of the longer lines are parallel (Do the three longer lines all go in the same direction?). [In fact, all three lines are parallel.]

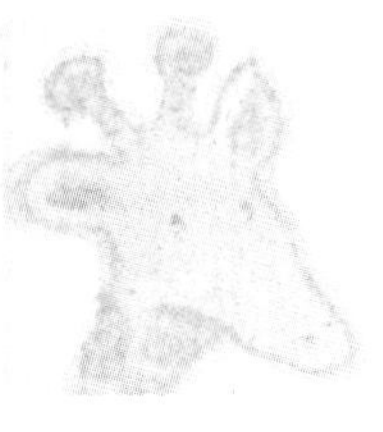

Diagram 4: Ask your students what this picture is a drawing of. [The drawing can be seen as a duck or as a rabbit. It is easier to see as a rabbit if you tilt it a little to the side.] This ambiguous figure, the duck/rabbit, is famous in philosophy because the philosopher Ludwig Wittgenstein discusses it in *Philosophical Investigations*, one of the most influential philosophy books of this century.

You could follow this activity up with other examples of optical illusions. Famous ones include the drawings of M. C. Escher, which children love to puzzle over. Another easy-to-create optical illusion is the 'bent stick' illusion. A straight stick half in and half out of water appears to bend as it enters the water. You can easily do this in the classroom by having a glass half full of water with a pencil resting in it. Let the children look at the pencil through the side of the glass, and ask them what shape the pencil is. When they describe it as bent, let them take it out and look at it.

Diagram 1

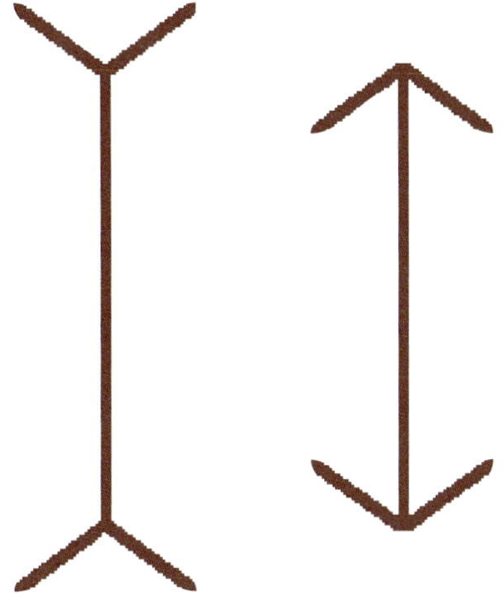

Diagram 2

Diagram 3

Diagram 4

Exercise: Things that are the way they appear

Gather together some objects, or pictures of objects, some of which might be said to appear to be something other than what they are (a list of some suggestions follows). Ask your students if they think that the appearance of each of them is the way it really is. Get them to explain their answer. Ask if everyone agrees.

1. a clown with a sad face
2. a toy truck
3. a picture of a lion
4. novelty items such as a pencil sharpener in the shape of an apple
5. a plastic flower
6. any item deliberately disguised as something else

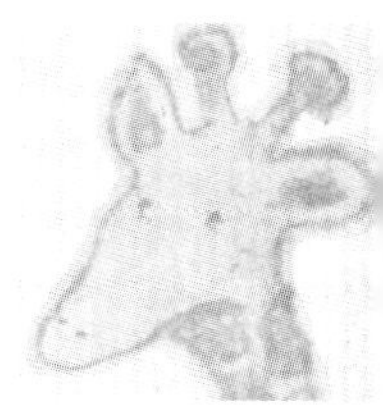

In a tree

In a tree a shining starling saw a long white line... and asked, «why do people need aeroplanes?» Another shining starling saw a big shadow... and wondered, «why do some birds prefer to be alone?» In a tree some shining starlings asked each other «do you think it would be better to nest elsewhere?» But a modern duck, overhearing the conversation, looked up and told the starlings that they had chosen the best site... for their particular network. In a tree a shining starling saw a long white line... and asked, «why do people need aeroplanes?» Another shining starling saw a big shadow... and wondered, «why do some birds prefer to be alone?» In a tree some shining starlings asked each other «do you think it would be better to nest elsewhere?» But a modern duck, overhearing the conversation, looked up and told the starlings that they had chosen the best site... for their particular network. In a tree a shining starling saw a long white line... and asked, «why do people need aeroplanes?» Another shining starling saw a big shadow... and wondered, «why do some birds prefer to be alone?» In a tree some shining starlings asked each other «do you think it would be better to nest elsewhere?» But a modern duck, overhearing the conversation, looked up and told the starlings that they had chosen the best site... for their particular network. In a tree a shining starling saw a long white line... and asked, «why do people need aeroplanes?» Another shining starling saw a big shadow... and wondered, «why do some birds prefer to be alone?» In a tree some shining starlings asked each other «do you think it would be better to nest elsewhere?» But a modern duck, overhearing the conversation, looked up and told the starlings that they had chosen the best site... for their particular network. In a tree a shining starling saw a long white line... and asked, «why do people need aeroplanes?» Another shining starling saw a big shadow... and wondered, «why do some birds prefer to be alone?» In a tree some shining starlings asked each other «do you think it would be better to nest elsewhere?» But a modern duck, overhearing the conversation, looked up and told the starlings that they had chosen the best site... for their particular network. In a tree a shining starling saw a long white line... and asked, «why do people need aeroplanes?» Another shining starling saw a big shadow... and wondered, «why do some birds prefer to be alone?» In a tree some shining starlings asked each other «do you think

Leading idea 1: Doing and inventing

One of the shining starlings asks 'Why do people need aeroplanes?'. Birds can fly naturally. Humans can also fly, but we are the only animal to fly that *can't* do it naturally. For most of the history of humanity, of course, we couldn't fly at all, but this didn't stop people dreaming of being able to.

In fact, humans are virtually the only animal that can find ways of doing things without being adapted by natural selection so as to be able to do them. For example, certain reptiles that 'saw' an ecological niche in the air evolved, first, leathery wings (like the Pterosaur) and eventually feathers, like the Archaeopteryx and the birds. Another example: birds (like ducks) that needed to swim evolved webbed feet, highly-oiled feathers and other features adapted to an aquatic environment.

It is for this reason that *Homo sapiens* is sometimes called 'the tool-using animal'. A few other animals can utilise naturally occurring objects, but only humans design and construct complex machines that use heavily modified materials in order to achieve feats way beyond their unaided abilities. Another way of putting this is to say that humans have to invent ways of doing things that animals achieve by evolution. We could say that humans *invent* aeroplanes, but birds have *become* aeroplanes! Instead of passing on these solutions to problems by genetic means, humans pass them on through a culture, using that most important of human inventions: language (see the next leading idea). [This discussion has drawn on Matthew Lipman's *Philosophical Inquiry*, p.172.]

Your students are likely to be able to come up with examples of animals that do seem to invent things: birds and nests; beavers and dams; spiders and webs; bees and hives (or even dances for showing the way to the flowers). It may well be interesting to explore the similarities and differences between such 'animal inventions' and 'human inventions'. Children, especially in the light of books (like this one!) that anthropomorphise animals, can be readier than adults to attribute to animals abilities that they may not really possess.

Some of these abilities can be made the subject of discussion. Do animals ever 'intend' to make things? Can they be said to 'design' things? Is the sort of knowledge that animals have the same as ours (which often seems to depend heavily on the ability to use words)? Can animals communicate ideas to one another, or is it only feelings and reactions? Many philosophers claim that the answer to all these questions must be 'no'. Even as famous a philosopher as René Descartes claimed that animals could not feel pain. But there are other philosophers who would argue that the matter is not so simple, and that some animals, particularly the higher mammals, have rudimentary abilities of these sorts.

Discussion plan: Doing and inventing

1. Why do people need aeroplanes?
2. Why don't shining starlings need aeroplanes?
3. Why do people need boats?
4. Why don't ducks need boats?
5. If people want to travel through the water, why don't they learn to swim?
6. If people want to travel through the air, why don't they learn to fly?
7. Could a duck build an aeroplane?
8. Can animals invent things?

Activity: Animal and human ways to do things

Divide the class into 'humans' and 'animals'. Tell them that you are going to give them each a task, and that they will have to draw the way they would get the task done. The 'humans' can only do things that ordinary humans are capable of doing, while the 'animals' can choose which kind of animal they want to be, but then can only do what an ordinary animal of that type can do.

Tasks:

1. Go from Melbourne to Devonport by sea.
2. Block up a stream to make a small lake.
3. Get a stick from the bottom of a river.
4. Go from Sydney to Canberra by air.
5. Push a large tree trunk.
6. Pick leaves from the top of a tall tree.

7. Make a hole in a tree trunk.
8. Dig a deep hole in the ground.
9. Swim very fast underwater.
10. Get from one side of a plain to the other very quickly.

Leading idea 2: Being alone and being together

The shining starlings are a very gregarious species — somewhat as humans are. Not all species like to live in a group, though. Hence the shining starling wonders why some birds prefer to be alone. Animals can derive many benefits from living in a group — protection against predators (e.g. herd animals), assistance in building things (e.g. rabbits building burrows), assistance in hunting (e.g. wolf packs) and so on.

We humans, however, gain a special advantage from living in groups. We have developed culture. Unlike animals, we pass on a great deal of knowledge through arguably our biggest advantage over other animals: language. The development of language is now thought to be due to the need for coordination between people owing to the close proximity in which humans live. Certainly, children who are denied close contact with others as they grow up fail to develop in many ways. In extreme cases, those children who are denied any exposure to language in their early years are never able to develop it. Thinking fits into the same category: indeed, the philosophy for children program is based on the understanding that exposure to, and participation in, thinking together aloud (through discussion) is essential to the development of thinking alone (in the head). This is why focused discussion within a class group is considered so important. [See also *Field* 8, *Tree* 6]

Children are often aware of the advantages and disadvantages of being on their own, and of being in a crowd. Giving children the opportunity to explore the pluses and minuses will enable them to become clearer about the role that others play in their lives. [See also *Path* 7, *Plain* 5]

Discussion plan: Alone and together

1. The shining starlings wonder why some birds prefer to be alone. Why do you think that these birds like being alone?
2. Why do you think that the shining starlings prefer to be together?
3. Are you more like the big bird or the shining starlings?
4. Do you like being alone sometimes? When?
5. Do you like being in a crowd sometimes? When?
6. Could you live entirely alone?

7. If you lived entirely on your own, what things would you be unable to do?
8. If you lived entirely on your own, what things would you miss?
9. Do you think that anyone could live entirely on their own?

Exercise: Things we do together

Ask your students to think about what effect it would have on the following if they were the only person in the world. Then ask them to think about the effect if they always had to be with other people and could never be alone.

1. the games you could play
2. the books you could read (or look at)
3. the food you would be able to eat
4. the things you could talk about
5. the things you could think about
6. the way you could think

Leading idea 3: Where do we belong?

The shining starlings ask each other whether it would be better to nest elsewhere. They look out of their nest at some wires, on which some other birds are sitting, and speculate about whether they would be better off nesting there. The shining starlings, of course, are well adapted to living in large groups in trees, as the duck is quick to point out to them. In general, animals are well adapted to their environment, having particular sorts of places where they live. Each of the books in this series is based around a particular type of animal and the habitat in which they are at home. Each of the animals has characteristics which fit it to the habitat.

Some animals are adapted for a wider range of environments than others. Humans, of course, live in a wider range of environments than any other creature on earth. The reason for this is linked to the ideas discussed in *Tree* 1: instead of adapting to new and different environments by changing our physical features, as most species do, humans have adapted by inventing various forms of new technology. These include such basics as clothing and shelter, as well as much more sophisticated devices such as heating systems and air-conditioning, or even space stations such as Mir.

In *Tree* 1, we were concerned with species. While children certainly need to be aware of humans as a species, their more pressing concern is likely to be where they personally belong. The children reading these books are likely to come from widely different physical environments. The variety of physical places that children could live in (or perhaps have lived in) links to the ideas discussed in the previous paragraph.

For most people, however, the social environment is much more important than the physical. Our social environment can also be looked at from several levels. At the most general level, we can talk about our culture. Where we belong is where we understand the culture, the customs and the expectations of the people with whom we live. A culture is, as the duck comments, a network (see *Tree* 6) in which we take our place. The extent to which we belong to a culture can be brought home to us quite forcefully if we go to live in a different culture (even if the physical environment is very similar), though young children will seldom have had this experience. Culture shock can be quite severe, as we find that nothing seems to happen in quite the same way we expect.

One of the arguments for multicultural education is that it enables children to have exposure to, and begin to understand, the different ways in which people from other cultures achieve common goals. Many of the ways in which we do things, which we take for granted, are specific to our culture, and could be done in many other ways. To become aware of this fact is to help make children more tolerant of others, more able to cope with change in their own lives, and (perhaps most importantly) better able to reflect on the things that they and those within their culture do. But multiculturalism should not be just an exercise in tolerance. Sometimes it is true that culturally different ways to do something are neither inherently better or worse than ours, sometimes it is not. Sometimes a judgement of better or worse is highly contentious.

Some examples. It would be hard to argue that (in general), eating with chopsticks is somehow better or worse than eating with a knife and fork. Of course, for particular dishes, one or the other might be superior (chopsticks for stir-fry, knife and fork for a roast). But is a culture that insists that girls (but not boys) must cover their faces in public better or worse than one that does not? Is a culture that routinely exhorts young children (through commercials) to eat nutritionally impoverished food better or worse than one that does not? As the examples show, it is not necessarily our culture which comes off better in these comparisons, but then neither is it always an open and shut case that one of the cultures is superior (consider these arguments: hiding girls' faces prevents their being judged solely on their looks; banning junk food advertising is a denial of free speech).

Finally, and probably most importantly to young children, there is the specific personal world to which they belong. Traditionally, this world includes mother, father and 1.5 siblings, as well as other relatives, friends, teachers, acquaintances (though we are increasingly sensitive to the fact that the details of this arrangement can vary to encompass one parent families, blended families etc.). It also includes familiar places: their room, home, school, neighbourhood and so on. To shift to a different family living in a nearby suburb would make little difference to either the geographic or the wider cultural environment, but it would be a major change for any young child.

But, of course, such changes do happen to children. Refugee children, the stolen generation of aboriginal children, orphans and others have experiences that involve changes as bad or worse than this. Children involved in marriage break-ups may be subject to most of them. Even children whose families relocate experience some of them. A few unfortunate children have home environments in which they do not feel that they belong, even in the absence of changes. For these reasons, discussion of 'where do we belong' needs to be undertaken with some sensitivity to those children in the class for whom such discussion might be traumatic.

This is not to say that the subject ought to be avoided: far from it. The fact that children are increasingly likely to be subject to such changes gives every reason for helping them to explore those things that they value most in their lives; those things that most make them feel that they do belong. Even children living in stressful circumstances can benefit from being able to discuss such ideas in a relatively safe and detached environment. But a community of inquiry in the classroom is not meant to be therapy, and teachers need to be alert to the possibility that some children might find such a discussion distressing, particularly if it starts to encourage disclosure of emotionally powerful material.

In discussing the feeling of belonging, we can explore those things that help to make us feel that we belong. A key concept here is likely to be familiarity. We know we belong when places, objects, people and ways of doing things are familiar to us. On the other hand, we are likely to feel out of place when things are unfamiliar. Of course, it usually only takes time and experience to make the unfamiliar familiar. It is no accident that the words 'family' and 'familiar' have the same root. For young children especially, the most familiar things are precisely those connected with the family. Often, a family member, or something connected with the family setting (a favourite soft toy, a piece of blanket) is enough to make even the most unfamiliar setting non-threatening.

Discussion plan: Belonging to a place

1. Where do the shining starlings belong?
2. Why do you think the shining starlings feel that they belong there?
3. Where does the duck belong?
4. Does a duck belong in the air or on the water, or some place else?
5. Do you belong at your house?

6. Would you belong at your house if there was different furniture in the house?
7. Would you belong at your house if there was a different family living in the house?
8. If you had to move to a different house, what would you take with you to make you feel that you belonged at the new house?

Activity: Where animals belong

Divide your class into groups of three or four. Tell them that you are going to give each group the name of an animal. They are to decide between them where their animal belongs, and then draw a picture of that animal in the place where it belongs. If they can think of several places where the animal belongs, they can draw a number of pictures, allocating a different picture to different members of the group. One member of the group, however, is to draw a picture of the animal in a place where it doesn't belong. When they have had time to draw their pictures, ask each group to show their pictures to the rest of the class and explain why they chose to draw the pictures they did. Encourage other class members to ask questions about, or comment on, the decisions that the group made.

Here is a list of possible animals: shining starlings, giraffes, snails, cows, tigers, dolphins, goldfish, eagles, monkeys, platypuses, koalas.

As a follow up, tell them that you are going to give them another animal. This time, make the animal human beings.

Exercise: Belonging to a culture

Act out (or show pictures of) each of the following, and ask your students to indicate whether they would feel that they belong. You might ask them to put thumbs up for 'yes', down for 'no' and sideways for 'not sure'. Ask a few of them to explain why they chose as they did.

You will need to obtain props for this exercise. Alternatively, you could gather appropriate pictures from magazines such as *National Geographic*.

Would you feel that you belonged in a place where …

1. many of the men wear hats like these? (Muslim or Jewish skull caps)
2. many of the women wear jewellery like this? (show a wedding or other ring on a finger)
3. a lot of the children wear scarves like these? (put on a scarf for a popular local football or other sporting team)
4. many of the women wear a scarf like this? (wrap a scarf around your head so only your eyes show)
5. people usually eat with these? (produce some chopsticks and pretend to eat with them)
6. people usually eat with these? (produce a knife and fork and pretend to eat with them)
7. people usually greet you like this? (pretend to hug another person and kiss them on both cheeks, European style — or do it to a child if you dare to, in this climate of non-touching of children)
8. people usually greet you like this? (bow with hands clasped, Japanese-style, looking at the floor, not the person greeted)
9. people usually greet you like this? (greet a child in your normal style)

Leading idea 4: Asking each other

The shining starlings ask each other questions. When we converse together, we can talk by making statements to each other and by asking questions of each other. Of course, there are other sorts of utterances, such as the 'go on' noises ('uhuh' etc.) or exclamations ('Wow!'), but questions and statements seem to make up the bulk of many conversations. Questions are less common than statements, in many types of conversations. In a typical classroom conversation between a teacher and a class of children, on the other hand, it is not true that statements outnumber questions, but it is not the children who are asking the questions.

In the Introduction and *Field* 1, we have noted some different types of questions. We would like to suggest here that two aspects of questions are important. Certainly, children ought to learn how to ask more questions, particularly more 'invitation to inquiry' questions. Every time you have asked your students to tell you their questions about the books you have been reading to them, you have been encouraging this. But in addition, children ought to discuss the nature and importance of questions themselves. In these discussions, they can distinguish between different types of questions and the uses to which they can be put. This is an example of the way that, in a community of inquiry, children (with the assistance of the teacher) can turn the investigation back onto the very tools of inquiry themselves. This enables the children to improve their control over, and use of, these tools.

Discussion plan: Questioning each other

1. Why do the shining starlings talk to each other?
2. Why do the shining starlings ask each other questions?
3. Do you ever ask a question when you are talking to other people?
4. What would life be like if you could never ask another question?
5. Why do we ask questions?
6. Do you ever ask a question, but not expect an answer? Can you give an example?
7. Do you ever ask a question when you know the answer already? Why?
8. Are the questions your friends ask you different from the questions your teacher asks you? In what way?
9. Are the questions your parents ask you more like the questions your friends ask, or the ones your teacher asks?

Activity: Asking each other

Divide your class into pairs. Give each pair a card with two roles on it, as suggested below. In each pair, one child takes on the first role, while the other child becomes the second. Each one has to think up several questions (the number depending on their age) to ask the other. If these two could talk to each other, what questions do you think they would ask each other?

Suggested pairs (think up your own too):

1. cat and mouse
2. dog and flea
3. duck and water
4. horse and rider
5. car and driver
6. pencil and paper
7. artist and painting
8. head and hat
9. hand and glove
10. candle and flame
11. teeth and tongue
12. mind and brain

Leading idea 5: Best

In response to their question, the duck informs the shining starlings that they have chosen the best site for their network. Deciding that something is the best might seem straightforward, but in many cases it isn't. Deciding who is the best runner in your class might seem easy — just have a race and see who wins. But even this is not so easy. How long should the race be? A child who will win a very short race might not win a long one. What sort of ground ought it to be over? The fastest runner on a track may not be fastest if the ground is uneven. Or maybe what we mean by best runner isn't the fastest, in any case. Maybe we mean the one that has the best running style, because we are looking for a runner to act as a model for our young runners. This would make the task much more difficult, because style seems even harder to judge than speed. Different people would value different things in a running style.

Let's see what we can gain from our example. A judgement as to the best always requires criteria against which to judge. Before we can make a judgement that something is the best, we need to decide the criterion for best that we are going to use. In complex situations, such as deciding which child is the best student, this can be very difficult, as teachers know. There may be many criteria which we want to use simultaneously, and then we have the added problem of knowing what weight to give to the different criteria. Which criteria are going to be chosen also depends on the context in which we are deciding the best, or the purpose for which we are choosing the best. Often which criteria will be considered to be most important also depends on the particular persons who are making the judgements. Such an analysis might seem too complex for young children. But criteria are just reasons for judgements, and children can be asked to give their reasons when they make judgements. If there are many criteria, children can give a number of reasons. Even the term 'criterion' can be introduced to quite young children: to them, it is just another word they are learning to use.

Exercise: The best

This is a task that you could give your class in small groups, provided that you have a child in every group who can read the criteria, or enough helpers to assist the children to read them.

If you were trying to find the person who could draw the best picture of a chair in your class, which of the following criteria would you think most important? Why? Can you put them in order from the most important to the least important?

1. how fast they could draw
2. how pretty the drawing was
3. how much you liked the person doing the drawing
4. what you had for breakfast that morning
5. how big their drawing was
6. whether the colours on the drawing look like the colours of the chair
7. how much like the shape of the chair the drawing was
8. whether you could sit on their drawing

Discussion plan: The best place to live

1. The duck said the shining starlings had chosen the best site for their network. Where was this best place? Do you think he was right?
2. What made the tree the best place for their network? Why was it better than the wires?
3. Would it be the best place for the duck to live? Why?
4. Would it be the best place for you to live? Why?
5. What would make one place better for you to live than another?
6. Is there one place that is the best place of all to live?

Activity: Mine is better than yours

The teacher starts by saying 'My pencil is the best because it is blue' (or something similar). A child has to say 'No, my pencil is better because …', supplying a reason why it is better. When several children have had a turn, ask the others to vote which reason was the best. Pick out a few voters to explain why they found that reason the best. Then start with a new object and reason.

Leading idea 6: Networks and communities

If you have been discussing the books in the order presented here, then you will be well on the way toward creating a community (we might say 'network') of inquiry in your classroom by now. Now might be a good time to talk with your students about how the community has been building up, and what makes it different from other things that happen in your class.

It is a good opportunity for you to think about the community too. What changes have you noticed? How do they fit with what you had hoped to get out of doing this with your class? How have the children surprised you? Have you had any disappointments?

Discussion plan: Networks and communities

1. Why does the duck call the shining starlings' tree a network?
2. What is a net? Is it like a conversation? How?
3. The story says the shining starlings live in a community. Is a network like a community? How?
4. Is this discussion you are having like a network? In what ways?
5. Is this group you are in now like a community? In what ways?
6. Do you have to agree with everyone else in a community?
7. Do you have to listen to everyone else in a community?
8. Do you have to like every one else in a community?
9. Do you have to think the same way as everyone else in a community?

Exercise: Our community

Ask your students to react to the following statements as you read them out, by holding their thumbs up if they agree, down if they disagree and sideways if they are not sure. After each statement, ask a few children to explain their decision.

When we discuss these books, we are forming a network or community of our own. In our community, we …

	Agree	Disagree
1. try to give a reason when we say something.		
2. shout out loud to be heard.		
3. never find an answer to anything.		
4. learn about what other people think.		
5. all get a chance to say something when we want.		
6. have a lot of fun.		
7. make sure that we understand what other people are saying.		
8. talk to our friend while someone else is saying something.		
9. ask lots of questions.		
10. stop listening when someone says something we don't agree with.		
11. try to show that what someone else said is wrong.		
12. learn how to work things out by talking together.		
13. think hard about things.		

Leading idea 7: Reading pictures

In a number of places throughout this manual, we have identified places where questions will be raised by the pictures, either in conjunction with, or instead of, the text. In picture books, the illustrations serve an equally important role in conveying the story and ideas as the text does. Children learn to 'read' pictures just as they learn to read words. This section addresses visual literacy, though not specifically in connection with *In a tree*.

Aesthetics

One of the first things that people often feel when they see a picture is a sense of appreciation (or otherwise) of the beauty in the picture. Your students are likely to make comments about pictures in these books too. Instead of always saying something like 'Yes, I think it's very nice, too', you can engage the class in a discussion about what makes a picture pretty, or striking, or beautiful or even ugly, if those are the terms in which the picture is described. While it is not always easy to put aesthetic feelings into words, nor is it always easy to give reasons for why we feel that way, they are open to discussion and reason. We can identify factors that are pleasing to the eye, and those that are not. Indeed, we can discuss whether the beauty in a picture is only about how it affects the eye, or whether it affects other parts of us as well.

Critics, of course, use criteria to judge art — the two words are clearly from the same root (the Greek *krites* = judge, in fact). But criteria for art cannot be applied in a mechanical way — 10 per cent to colour, 20 per cent to form etc. First, the interactions between aspects (colour and form, for example) are complex. Secondly, personal taste plays a big part in our appreciation of art, and personal taste is heavily influenced by our personal history.

Nevertheless, an important part of art education is to assist children to become aware of these different aspects of a work of art. While practical art education can help children to master the technical aspects of the criteria of beauty, the philosophy of art can help us to discuss the nature of the criteria themselves. Aesthetics is the branch of philosophy concerned with questions of beauty. The discussion plan below can make a start on this, by addressing the relatively simpler criteria of shape (form), unity, colour and content [see also *Field* 2, *Path* 2]. These are not all the aesthetic criteria, and it is possible a child might mention another — texture, maybe, or intensity, or impact. If so, use the pattern below to try to address it as well.

Discussion Plan: Criteria for good pictures

[*Note:* Each of the following questions can be slanted towards a work of art the child likes or dislikes. For convenience, we will not use the 'dislikes' alternatives, but your questions can be targeted either way.]

1. Why do you think the picture is good (beautiful, pretty)?
2. Would you like the picture less if the shapes used in it were different? What sorts of shapes would look worse? Why do you think so? What makes a shape pleasing?
3. Does the picture go together, or do some parts of it look out of place? Do you think the picture would not be as good if it had a Christmas tree in it? How can we tell if things go together in a picture? Are all pictures where things don't go together well, bad pictures?
4. Would you like the picture as much if the illustrator had chosen different colours? What colour would be worse, and what would it be used to colour? Are all drawings with pretty colours, beautiful drawings? Are all drawings with ugly colours, bad drawings? What makes a colour beautiful, anyway? [Ask a child to point to a beautiful colour somewhere in the room.] Do you all agree that this colour is beautiful? Why?
5. Is part of what you like about that picture something which is in it? Which thing? Why do you like that bit? Could you have a beautiful picture about something that isn't very nice? Could you have an ugly picture about something you like a lot? Could there be a nice picture about nothing at all? What might it look like?

Activity: Good and bad pictures

Give the children plenty of drawing materials. Tell them that you are going to ask them to draw two drawings. They can choose what the drawings will be about, but one of the drawings has to be just like the other, except for one thing. One of them must be more beautiful than the other. The only thing that they can change to make one more beautiful than the other is the colours that they use. Everything else about the drawing, they should try to make as much alike as they can. (For younger children, you might use a colouring-in drawing).

If this works well, then maybe you can try some more ambitious variations. Ask them to draw the same object using the same colours, but use a more beautiful and less beautiful shape. Alternatively, they could add something to a drawing they have done that will make it less beautiful because it doesn't fit in well.

It would be a nice idea to talk about some of the pairs of pictures with the class. Ask for volunteers, and show their picture pair. Ask the rest of the class to judge which is the more beautiful one, before the artist identifies them. With a bit of luck, you'll have some disagreement, and be able to discuss why people have different ideas about beauty.

Book design

The artists for these books made a large number of decisions about how to present their work. Some of these can be recognised by the children, if they look carefully at the illustrations. How did the artists give a unity to each of the books, and to the series as a whole? What stylistic decisions did they make? Some of these questions might arise when children comment on, or raise questions about, the illustrations.

The activity suggested below requires a degree of sophistication in design matters. It is probably best done with older children, who have perhaps tried to write their own picture books.

Activity: Design jigsaw

A. Split the children into groups, so that each group can have a copy of one of the books to look at. Each person in a group has to become an 'expert'on the design of the book. Ask the children to look at the illustrations and think:

1. What things look the same on every page of the book?
2. What things look different from page to page?
3. What is the relationship between each page and the next page?
4. How far do the pictures go — one page, both pages (double spread), more than two pages?

B. After the groups have had sufficient time to think about and discuss their book, send one member of each group to a new group (that is, the new groups will each be made up of four members, one each of whom is an expert on one of the books). Each of the members explains to the others what they have found out about his/her book. The copies of the books can be passed from group to group, so the expert has her/his book to show the others.

C. Once each expert has explained their book, then the whole group can consider the ways in which the books are the same and different.

Appendices

Lipman, Matthew. (1978)Suki. Montclair, N.J.: First Mountain Foundation for the Institute for the Advancement of Philosophy for Children, Montclair State College. Plus Lipman, Matthew & Sharp, Ann Margaret. (1980)Writing: How and why: instructional manual to accompany Suki. Montclair, N.J.: Institute for the Advancement of Philosophy for Children. [Years 8 - 10] Lipman, Matthew. (1980)Mark. Montclair, N.J.: First Mountain Foundation for the Institute for the Advancement of Philosophy for Children, Montclair State College. Plus Lipman, Matthew & Sharp, Ann Margaret. (1980) Social Inquiry: instructional manual to accompany Mark. Lanham, MD: University Press of America. [Years 10 - 12]. Lipman, Matthew. (1978)Suki. Montclair, N.J.: First Mountain Foundation for the Institute for the Advancement of Philosophy for Children, Montclair State College. Plus Lipman, Matthew & Sharp, Ann Margaret. (1980)Writing: How and why: instructional manual to accompany Suki. Montclair, N.J.: Institute for the Advancement of Philosophy for Children. [Years 8 - 10]. Lipman, Matthew. (1980)Mark. Montclair, N.J.: First Mountain Foundation for the Institute for the Advancement of Philosophy for Children, Montclair State College. Plus Lipman, Matthew & Sharp, Ann Margaret. (1980) Social Inquiry: instructional manual to accompany Mark. Lanham, MD: University Press of America. [Years 10 - 12]. Lipman, Matthew. (1978)Suki. Montclair, N.J.: First Mountain Foundation for the Institute for the Advancement of Philosophy for Children, Montclair State College. Plus Lipman, Matthew & Sharp, Ann Margaret. (1980)Writing: How and why: instructional manual to accompany Suki. Montclair, N.J.: Institute for the Advancement of Philosophy for Children. [Years 8 - 10]. Lipman, Matthew. (1980)Mark. Montclair, N.J.: First Mountain Foundation for the Institute for the Advancement of Philosophy for Children, Montclair State College. Plus Lipman, Matthew & Sharp, Ann Margaret. (1980) Social Inquiry: instructional manual to accompany Mark. Lanham, MD: University Press of America. [Years 10 - 12]. Lipman, Matthew. (1978)Suki. Montclair, N.J.: First Mountain Foundation for the Institute for the Advancement of Philosophy for Children, Montclair State College. Plus Lipman, Matthew & Sharp, Ann Margaret. (1980)Writing: How and why: instructional manual to accompany Suki. Montclair, N.J.: Institute for the Advancement of Philosophy for Children. [Years 8 - 10]. Lipman, Matthew. (1980)Mark. Montclair, N.J.: First Mountain Foundation for the Institute for the Advancement of Philosophy for Children, Montclair State College. Plus Lipman, Matthew & Sharp, Ann Margaret. (1980) Social Inquiry: instructional manual to accompany Mark. Lanham, MD: University Press of America. [Years 10 - 12]. Lipman, Matthew. (1978)Suki. Montclair, N.J.: First Mountain Foundation for the Institute for the Advancement of Philosophy for Children, Montclair State College. Plus Lipman, Matthew & Sharp, Ann Margaret. (1980)Writing: How and why: instructional manual to accompany Suki. Montclair,

Contacts for Philosophy for Children

For information about programs, workshops and other activities relating to Philosophy for Children, and for information about Philosophy for Children organisations in local areas, contact:

The Centre for Philosophy for Children
ACER
Private Bag 55
Camberwell
Victoria 3124
Australia

Phone + 61 3 9277 5594
FAX + 61 3 9277 5500
E-mail: splitter@acer.edu.au

Books for further reading

Classroom materials (Australian)

Abbott, Colleen & Wilks, Susan. (1997) *Thinking and talking through literature*. Highett, Vic.: Hawker Brownlow Education. [Years 5 - 8]

Cam, Philip. (1993, 1994, 1997 respectively) *Thinking stories 1, 2 and 3: Philosophical inquiry for children*. Plus teacher resource/activity books for each. (Illustrations by Ken and Karen Rinkel). Sydney: Hale & Iremonger. [Years 5 - 8]

De Haan, Chris, MacColl, San & McCutcheon, Lucy. (1995) *Philosophy with kids*. Books 1 to 4. Melbourne: Longman. [Kinder - Year 2]

Keen, Judy. (1997) *Brain strain 1 and 2*. Three booklets in each set: short stories, big format pictures and teacher resource. Melbourne: Macmillan Education. [Years 5 - 8]

Parker, Michael. (1997) *The quest for the stone of wisdom*. Sydney: Scholastic. [Years 7 - 10]

Sprod, Tim. (1993) *Books into ideas*. Cheltenham, Vic.: Hawker Brownlow Education. [Kinder - Year 2]

Classroom materials (International)

Lipman, Matthew. (1978) *Suki*. Montclair, N.J.: First Mountain Foundation for the Institute for the Advancement of Philosophy for Children, Montclair State College. Plus Lipman, Matthew & Sharp, Ann Margaret. (1980) *Writing: How and why*: instructional manual to accompany Suki. Montclair, N.J.: Institute for the Advancement of Philosophy for Children. [Years 8 - 10]

Lipman, Matthew. (1980) *Mark*. Montclair, N.J.: First Mountain Foundation for the Institute for the Advancement of Philosophy for Children, Montclair State College. Plus Lipman, Matthew & Sharp, Ann Margaret. (1980) *Social inquiry*: instructional manual to accompany Mark. Lanham, MD: University Press of America. [Years 10 - 12]

Lipman, Matthew. (1981) *Pixie*. Montclair, N.J.: First Mountain Foundation for the Institute for the Advancement of Philosophy for Children, Montclair State College. Plus Lipman, Matthew & Sharp, Ann Margaret. (1984) *Looking for Meaning*: instructional manual to accompany Pixie. Lanham, MD: University Press of America, [Years 3 - 6]

Lipman, Matthew. (1983) *Lisa*. Lanham: University Press of America. Plus Lipman, Matthew & Sharp, Ann Margaret. (1983) *Ethical Inquiry*: instructional manual to accompany Lisa (Lanham, MD: University Press of America. [Years 7 - 9]

Lipman, Matthew. (1986) *Kio and Gus*. Rev. ed. Upper Montclair, N.J.: First Mountain Foundation, for the Institute for the Advancement of Philosophy for Children, Montclair State College. Plus Lipman, Matthew & Sharp, Ann Margaret. (1986) *Wondering at the world*: instructional manual to accompany Kio and Gus. Lanham, MD: University Press of America. [Years 3 - 5]

Lipman, Matthew. (1988) *Elfie*. Upper Montclair, N.J.: Institute for the Advancement of Philosophy for Children. Plus Lipman, Matthew & Gazzar Ann. *Getting our thoughts together*: instructional manual to accompany Elfie. [Kinder - Year 2]

Lipman, Matthew. (1992) *Harry Stottlemeier's discovery*. [Australian adaptation prepared by Laurance Splitter]. Melbourne, Vic.: ACER, Plus Lipman, Matthew, Sharp, Ann Margaret & Oscanyan, Frederick S. (eds). (1984) *Philosophical inquiry*: an instructional manual to accompany Harry Stottlemeier's discovery. 2nd ed. Lanham, MD: University Press of America, [Years 6 - 8]

Murris, Karin. (1992) *Teaching philosophy with picture books*. London: Infonet Publications. [Kinder - Year 2]

Further references

Cam, Philip. (1995) *Thinking together: Philosophical inquiry for the classroom*. Sydney: Primary English Teaching Association and Hale & Iremonger.

Carey, Susan. (1985) *Conceptual change in childhood*. Cambridge MA: MIT Press.

Dillon, J T. (1994) *Using discussion in classrooms*. Buckingham, England: Open University Press.

Lipman, Matthew & Sharp, Ann Margaret. (eds). (1994) *Growing up with philosophy*. Dubuque, Iowa: Kendall/Hunt.

Lipman, Matthew, Sharp, Ann Margaret & Oscanyan, Frederick S. (1980) *Philosophy in the classroom*. 2nd ed. Philadelphia: Temple U. P.

Lipman, Matthew. (1988) *Philosophy goes to school*. Philadelphia: Temple U. P.

Lipman, Matthew. (1991) *Thinking in education*. Cambridge: Cambridge U. P.

Lipman, Matthew (ed). (1993) *Thinking children and education*. Dubuque, Iowa: Kendall/Hunt.

Matthews, Gareth. (1980) *Philosophy and the young child*. Cambridge, MA: Harvard University Press.

Matthews, Gareth. (1984) *Dialogues with children*. Cambridge, MA: Harvard University Press.

Matthews, Gareth. (1994) *Philosophy of childhood*. Cambridge, MA: Harvard University Press.

Pritchard, Michael. (1996) *Reasonable children: Moral education and moral learning*. Lawrence: University Press of Kansas.

Reed, Ron. (1983) *Talking with children*. Denver, Colorado: Arden Press.

Reed, Ron. (1992) *When we talk*. Fort Worth, Texas: Analytic Teaching Press.

Sharp, Ann Margaret & Reed, Ron. (1992) *Studies in philosophy for children: Harry Stottlemeier's discovery*. Philadelphia: Temple U. P.

Sharp, Ann Margaret & Reed, Ron. (1995) *Studies in philosophy for children: Pixie*. Madrid: De La Torre.

Splitter, Laurance & Sharp, Ann Margaret. (1995) *Teaching for better thinking: The classroom community of inquiry*. Melbourne: Australian Council for Educational Research.

Wilks, Sue. (1995) *Critical and creative thinking: Strategies for classroom inquiry*. Armadale, Vic: Eleanor Curtain.